THE UNEXPECTED UNIVERSE OF DORIS LESSING

Rece
Con
Serie

The
Robe

Cloc
Rich

Aper
Bria

The
A Cri
Don

The S
Select
the Fa
Rober

Death
Carl

The T
Fictio
Rober

The R
Moder
Raym

The C
Don D

The S
Litera
on the
Rober

Some
Thom

THE UNEXPECTED UNIVERSE OF DORIS LESSING

A STUDY IN NARRATIVE TECHNIQUE

KATHERINE FISHBURN

CONTRIBUTIONS TO THE STUDY OF SCIENCE
FICTION AND FANTASY, NUMBER 17

GREENWOOD PRESS
WESTPORT, CONNECTICUT • LONDON, ENGLAND

Library of Congress Cataloging in Publication Data

Fishburn, Katherine, 1944-
  The unexpected universe of Doris Lessing.

  (Contributions to the study of science fiction and
fantasy, ISSN 0193-6875 ; no. 17)
  Bibliography: p.
  Includes index.
  1. Lessing, Doris May, 1919-   —Criticism and
interpretation. 2. Science fiction, English—History
and criticism. I. Title. II. Series.
PR6023.E833Z66 1985   823'.914   85-9913
ISBN 0-313-23424-8 (lib. bdg. : alk. paper)

Library of Congress Catalog Card Number: 85-9913
ISBN: 0-313-23424-8
ISSN: 0193-6875

First published in 1985

Greenwood Press
A division of Congressional Information Service, Inc.
88 Post Road West
Westport, Connecticut 06881

Printed in the United States of America

The paper used in this book complies with the
Permanent Paper Standard issued by the National
Information Standards Organization (Z39.48-1984).

10 9 8 7 6 5 4 3 2 1

Copyright Acknowledgments

Grateful acknowledgment is given to Alfred A. Knopf, Inc., for permission to re-
print from the following titles by Doris Lessing: *Briefing for a Descent into Hell*,
copyright 1971; *The Memoirs of a Survivor*, copyright 1974; *Re: Colonised Planet 5,
Shikasta*, copyright 1979; *The Marriages Between Zones Three, Four, and Five*,
copyright 1980; *The Sirian Experiments*, copyright 1981; *The Making of the Representative for Planet 8*, copyright 1982; *The Sentimental Agents*, copyright 1983.

To Tom
Heard melodies are sweet,
but those unheard
Are sweeter.

Contents

Acknowledgments

For providing me with a forum to exchange news and ideas, I am grateful to the members of the Doris Lessing Society.

For helping me work out some of these ideas and for his habit of leaving interesting books all over our office, Jim Seaton deserves special recognition.

For their own work on Lessing and the support and encouragement they have given mine over the years, Betsy Draine, Ellen Cronan Rose, Claire Sprague, and Paul Schlueter deserve special thanks.

For everything she has done on my behalf in the past several years, my editor Maureen Melino also deserves special thanks.

For her loyal friendship, enthusiastic reception of my ideas, and outrageous sense of humor, June Jacobson has both my gratitude and my love.

For permission to reproduce his painting "What god shall we adore?", I am especially grateful to DeWitt Cheng.

Finally, and above all, I wish to thank Tom for putting up with me for the two years it took to write this book. Life has never been better.

If you do not expect it, you will not find the unexpected, for it is hard to find and difficult.

—Heraclitus

Our identity is a dream. We are process, not reality, for reality is an illusion of the daylight—the light of our particular day.

—Loren Eiseley

Introduction:
Transforming the World

Although Doris Lessing was officially a member of the Communist Party for only a short period of time, this temporary affiliation seems to have had a lasting impact on her writing—especially her science fiction. The impact is most evident here, I would suggest, because it is in her science fiction that Lessing sets out most clearly to critique modern social and political structures. It is true, of course, that social criticism has never been absent from her fiction, appearing as it does in one form or another in all her novels, from *The Grass Is Singing* (1950) to *The Diaries of Jane Somers* (1984). At the same time its relative importance has fluctuated widely. In her earlier fiction, for example, Lessing channels most of her social criticism through her characters. If the balance between story and message tilts here, it is usually in favor of the story. In her science fiction, on the other hand, she shifts her attention more to her message.[1] This shift is accompanied by her narrators' rise to prominence. By thus subordinating her characters to the voice of her narrator, Lessing implies that it is time for her to address us more directly—before it is too late.

But even in her urge to speak directly, she never falls into the trap that proved so fatal to the proletarian novelists of the 1930s and 1940s. That is to say, although Lessing may on occasion preach, as a rule she doesn't allow her political purposes to overwhelm her aesthetic ethos. Unlike these writers, whom she identifies in "The

Small Personal Voice" ("SPV") as having given protest literature a bad name, Lessing herself is not writing Party propaganda.[2] Although she is a self-proclaimed socially committed writer, she is not committed to Marxism or any other political party. She is committed, instead, to other people—to being a positive "instrument of change" in their lives ("SPV," 190). Missing from her fiction, therefore, are the political dogma and Marxist blueprints that make most protest literature nothing more than what she calls "simple tracts about factories or strikes or economic injustice" ("SPV," 187). No doubt, if one were so inclined, one could cite passages where her didacticism has got the better of her art. But in the main her writing provides us with that intellectual resting point she so idealizes in "The Small Personal Voice"—that point between philosophical extremes where, having defined the alternatives, she leaves it to her readers to choose for themselves ("SPV," 194).

As I implied above, the problems she presents us with in her science fiction have less to do with character than with narrative process. Unlike her earlier fiction, her science fiction involves us primarily in the ideas and intricacies of the texts—texts which have as their purpose the transformation of reality itself. To understand this difference, the distinction that Sheldon Sacks makes between "represented actions" and "apologues" is helpful here. According to Sacks, in represented actions (such as Lessing's earlier works) the focus is on characters and their impact on us; in this kind of fiction, therefore, "the most intellectual belief, the most extended social criticism, the most penetrating ethical comment, become integral parts of a whole work only as they move us to the appropriate response to the created characters."[3] But in an apologue, on the other hand, "the most poignant experience, the most subtly created character, the most eloquent prose, become integral parts of a complete work only as they move us to some realization—implicit or formulated—about the world external to the literary creation" (Sacks, 277). In the case of Lessing's science fiction, the text confronts us with the problem of alien realities and unknown worlds which we try to understand on the basis of what we already know about the universe. Having engaged our imaginative and cognitive thought processes in this dialectical exchange, the text then throws us back on the world as it were—with the expectation that we will no longer perceive it as before. In short, Lessing uses the conventions of science fiction and Marxist social criticism to help us transcend the limitations of known reality.

As well matched as Lessing's work shows science fiction and Marxism to be, their intellectual compatibility has not always been immediately apparent. Because of its desire to provide an objective scientific analysis of society, for example, Marxism has generally been quite skeptical of utopian literature. But as Tom Kitwood argues in " 'Science' and 'Utopia' in the Marxist Tradition," the time has long since passed when we could consider science to be either wholly objective or value-free. Instead, given its extraordinary influence in our culture, we would do better to consider it an ideology in its own right—one that in Kitwood's view "expresses, in an idealized and mystified form, the structures of capitalism and technocracy."[4] At the same time that science has lost its claim to objectivity, utopianism has lost its stigma of impracticality—largely because of the advances in science and technology. This leaves Kitwood believing that utopianism should be regarded as a "necessary part of any practical program of social change which draws its main insights from realist social analysis" (Kitwood, 40). As reasonable as Kitwood's position is, Marxist thought has been slow to change on this issue. Thus it is not surprising that nearly ten years before Kitwood, Herbert Marcuse was defending utopian art on the basis of its ability to help us "break with the familiar, the routine ways of seeing, hearing, feeling, understanding things [and] become receptive to the potential forms of a nonaggressive, nonexploitative world."[5] Convinced that utopias are no longer impossible to realize, Marcuse urges us to consider utopian thought as a possible bridge to a new way of seeing and thinking. In his own utopian vision, in fact, he imagines a time when science and technology have been mobilized to create a new society based on life-affirming needs. As a result of this change, "Technique would . . . tend to become art, and art would tend to form reality: the opposition between imagination and reason, higher and lower facilities, poetic and scientific thought, would be invalidated" (*Essay*, 24). Before this reconciliation can be achieved, however, technological and scientific goals must be redirected, and the language must be freed of its distortions; in short, a new sensibility must emerge that in turn will free and feed the imagination in its efforts to reconstruct reality. In this comprehensive transformation

of known reality, science fiction—whether utopian or apocalyptic—can play a crucial role, especially when it is in the hands of a
Merlin like Lessing.

Although in retrospect Lessing's own journey to science fiction
has a certain logic to it, it is not something that necessarily could
have been foreseen. When she described her goals for herself as a
writer in "The Small Personal Voice," for example, she identified
the nineteenth-century novel as the "highest point of literature" and
the realistic novel as the "highest form of prose writing; higher
than and out of the reach of any comparison with expressionism, impressionism, symbolism, naturalism, or any other ism" ("SPV,"
188). Realism she describes as "art which springs so vigorously and
naturally from a strongly-held, though not necessarily intellectually-
defined, view of life that it absorbs symbolism" (188). Through
such high praise of the genre, Lessing implied that it was realism
that held the key to the effective social change she hoped to bring
about through her own writing. But as much as she might have admired realism in 1957, she soon found it unsuitable for what she
wanted to accomplish, which was a significant if not total transformation of the way her audience viewed the world itself. Although
she continues to write realism (as evidenced by her most recent
work, *The Diaries of Jane Somers*), from the early seventies to the
mid-eighties her interest clearly lay elsewhere. By the time she published the first installment of her *Canopus in Argos: Archives*
series, in fact, her complex narrative technique had come to dominate her characters, leading us to the inevitable conclusion that the
meaning of *Shikasta* lies less in them than it does in the structure itself—hardly qualifying this novel as an example of the "highest
form of prose writing" that Lessing so praised nearly thirty years
ago.

I must interject here that I do not want it thought that I am trying
in the 1980s to hold Lessing to the standards for fiction she seemed
to set for herself as a goal in 1957. To do so would be blind to the
fact that authors can and do change over a lifetime of writing. It
would also be a criticism sorely out of date, as Lessing seemed to be
dissatisfied with these standards as early as 1962 if the shape of *The
Golden Notebook* is any indication of her attitude on the question
of realistic fiction. What I am trying to do, however, is suggest that
even though her artistic techniques might have changed in thirty

years, her artistic commitment has remained constant. I am suggesting that in her science fiction Lessing has found a new vehicle to transmit the same philosophical principles she described in 1957 and apparently still adheres to—those dealing with the social responsibility of the artist. I am also suggesting that her decision to forego the realistic novel was not an easy one for her, that before she was comfortable about the decision she experimented with various modifications of realism.[6] A brief look at the last few novels she published before *Shikasta* should support my point.

In 1969 she published *The Four-Gated City*, concluding her epic five-volume *Children of Violence* series. This novel focuses on Martha Quest and several other people who live in London in the half a century following the end of World War II. Although *The Four-Gated City*, structurally speaking, looks fairly conventional, some quite unconventional things begin to happen to Martha—the kind of things that violate what we know of reality. These extraordinary changes in Martha's perceptual capabilities and the apocalyptic conclusion to the novel itself strongly suggest that Lessing was letting go of realism—certainly realism as we would normally define it. This impression is further confirmed, of course, in *Briefing for a Descent into Hell*, which combines an interest in character with structural experimentation and an emphasis on utterly fantastic events. In fact, this novel, which was published in 1971, draws on such diverse literary traditions that critics have been uncertain whether to read it as psycho-drama or science fiction. Shortly after this formal experiment, Lessing returned again to realism in *The Summer Before the Dark.* In this 1973 novel she describes what it is like for a woman on the far side of middle age to confront the fact that she has been virtually a non-person all her life. Although the book is clearly an example of realism, much of its meaning is conveyed in a lengthy dream sequence—a fact that suggests Lessing's increasing interest in symbolism. And just one year later she published *The Memoirs of a Survivor*, which uses the persona of another middle-aged woman to predict the fall of Western civilization and introduce us to an imaginary universe. Like the three novels that preceded it, *Memoirs* is both a warning to us and a promise of better things to come if only we learn to mend our ways.

Clearly the content of these four novels is evidence of Lessing's ongoing commitment to her goal of social change. But just as clearly

their diverse structures suggest that in the ten-year period between
The Four-Gated City (1969) and *Shikasta* (1979) Lessing was
seeking alternative forms to realism that would best allow her to
maintain her artistic commitment to society. That she experimented
so widely suggests that she may have been having some difficulty
finding the particular genre best suited to her ideals. The kinds of difficulties she encountered may be explained in part by the ideas
found in Herbert Marcuse's earlier work *One-Dimensional Man*.
Like Lessing, Marcuse finds much to fault in modern industrial
society; like her he also believes that artists have a vital role to play
in reforming this society. The artistic *commitment* that Lessing
identifies as the goal of her writing, Marcuse describes as artistic
alienation. Although commitment and alienation appear to be
polar opposites, the opposition is only semantic in nature, as both
writers call for the artist to serve the needs of the people. Lessing
claims that at the very least an artist must recognize that "one is a
writer at all because one represents, makes articulate, is continuously
and invisibly fed by, numbers of people who are inarticulate, to
whom one belongs, to whom one is responsible" ("SPV," 201). In
One-Dimensional Man, Marcuse also calls for artists to be
responsible to society, but he views this responsibility from another
direction. For him, the function of the artist is to oppose the status
quo and the state—an opposition that implies a commitment to
those who are adversely affected by the status quo and who cannot
articulate (or perhaps even see) their subordination to the needs of
the state.

This function is particularly difficult to sustain, Marcuse argues,
in a society like ours which is notable for its thoroughgoing "integration of opposites." What is needed in such a society is the reintroduction of opposition, the reintroduction of conflict between
culture and society. The opposition is missing in the people themselves, Marcuse believes, because of the historically unprecedented
ability of the state to meet the physical needs of the masses.
Because people are so well off in this country, social "reality sur-
passes its culture"—that is, we have at our disposal anything we
might imagine we want, and more (Marcuse, 56). As a result of
living so well, we have seen a "flattening out of the antagonism between culture and social reality," which has taken place largely
through the "wholesale incorporation" of cultural values into the

"established order, through their reproduction and display on a massive scale" (Marcuse, 57). This is as true of our low culture as it is of our high culture. That is, the kind of opposition represented, for example, in the costumes worn by hippies or punks is quickly and greedily absorbed by Madison Avenue where it is transmuted into the latest clothing style for affluent middle-class adults and their children.

In contrast to this imitation alienation, the kind of genuine artistic alienation that Marcuse calls for can readily be found in the writings of those cultural subgroups who have traditionally been exempted from the mainstream of white, middle-class American life. Ever since 1963, when Betty Friedan published *The Feminine Mystique*, this chorus of protest has been amplified by the impassioned voices of angry women. In fact, the literature that now seems to speak out most eloquently against the status quo is that being written by women—women of color, women of the lower class, women who are feminists, lesbians, and political separatists.[8] Like the radical black writers of the 1960s, these women have had very little to say about Western culture that is positive. Not only do they criticize Western values and customs, but they also criticize the very language that has been used to preserve these customs. I am thinking here of writers like Mary Daly, Shulamith Firestone, Adrienne Rich, Barbara Smith, Sally Miller Gearhart, Suzy McKee Charnas, Cherríe Moraga, Gloria Anzaldúa, and Toni Cade Bambara—to name just a few.

Although Doris Lessing would never identify herself as a radical feminist writer, she does share many of the same political views as these women. And although she has been, by birth, a member of the elite white ruling class, she has always stood, by choice, in opposition to its nationalistic, imperialistic, and sexist policies. She expresses her political views not by attempting to restructure the language (although she is critical of it in more than one context) but by attempting to restructure thinking itself.[9] In attempting this, she has tried to restructure one of our most venerable cultural forms—that of the novel. Her most famous restructuring of it, coincidentally, is also her most feminist work—*The Golden Notebook*. But her most thorough restructuring of it, I would argue, is *Shikasta*. Here not only is she restructuring the fiction that is "the novel," but she is also restructuring the fiction that is our history. It is in science fiction, a form she has come to by circuitous routes, that she is able to oppose the politics of the status quo to best advantage and to affirm her commitment to the greater good of humanity.

As a social critic and a prophetic writer, Doris Lessing, like all true visionaries, has been faced with the eternal problem of how best to communicate her message to a world intellectually and temperamentally unprepared to listen to her. Many of those whom she would address through her fiction resist her message because what she has to say goes against what these people hold most sacred. Rather than supporting the Western ethos of individualism and pragmatism, for example, Lessing proffers an alternative ethos based on cooperation and transcendence—ideals found in much recent feminist science fiction such as Thea Alexander's *2150 A.D.* (1971) and Sally Miller Gearhart's *The Wanderground* (1979). In offering this alternative philosophy, Lessing warns us to forego our technological competitiveness and nationalistic hubris—showing us, as part of her argument, what will happen to us if we do not. By setting herself and her art in opposition to the nationalistic policies of the time, she reintroduces the dialectical tension between art and reality that Marcuse calls for in *One-Dimensional Man.* Like the feminist science fiction writers cited above, Lessing also uses the dialectics of her fiction as imaginative bridges to new worlds, thus lending support to Marcuse's ideas in *An Essay on Liberation.* In short, Lessing shares with these American social critics the desire to restructure the universe of discourse and with it the universe itself.

Discovering science fiction has brought her a kind of artistic liberation, as in it she says she has been "set free into a larger scope, with more capacious possibilities."[10] At the same time it has enabled her "to put questions" to herself and her readers and "to explore ideas and sociological possibilities."[11] In other words, she finds useful the uncommon content of science fiction and its formal characteristics, both of which force her and her readers into new ways of thinking about the universe.

Two descriptions of science fiction that shed light on Lessing's work are those by Robert Galbreath and Darko Suvin. In "Ambiguous Apocalypse," Robert Galbreath defines science fiction as being "essentially characterized by a significant concern . . . with contradictions of the consensus view of reality presumably held by author and reader alike—which are made credible by virtue of rationales derived from science, philosophy, psychology, religion, mythology, the occult, and other thought-structures, actual or invented. The effect is to challenge the reader's conceptions of reality; the basic function is epistemological."[12] Although Galbreath's definition describes Lessing's science fiction in general terms, in the final sentence he seems to pinpoint exactly what her work attempts, as Lessing is trying, perhaps above all, to modify the way we experience everyday reality. In his well-known history and taxonomy of the genre, *Metamorphoses of Science Fiction*, Darko Suvin defines it in the telling phrase "cognitive estrangement," by which he means that science fiction is based on extrapolations of known reality (its cognitive quality) and a process of making the familiar more visible by first making it strange (its quality of estrangement).[13] In the phrase "cognitive estrangement" Suvin has given us a shorthand description of what science fiction *is* and what it *does*—a description that also seems to sum up what Lessing's science fiction is and what it does.

Taking as my point of departure Suvin's definition, which itself is indebted to Victor Shklovsky's concept of "defamiliarization" and Bertolt Brecht's "estrangement effect," I find in Lessing's science fiction the complementary formal techniques of what I call "recognition" and "re-cognition."[14] By recognition I mean, much as Suvin and Shklovsky mean by their respective terms, that Lessing, through various narrative strategies, forces us to examine our everyday world from new perspectives. The term is meant to imply a cyclical movement or interrelated activity whereby Lessing and her readers are mutually engaged in modifying reality.[15] She is describing reality differently and we are learning to see it differently, events that suggest something of a dialogue between text and reader—and also a causal relationship between language and perception. Because we are learning to recognize ourselves in what are the alien worlds (alternate realities) of her texts, we are also changing our views of what the world is like; the more we read Lessing, therefore, the more we see the world through her eyes. Ultimately, if she is successful in breaking through our perceptual screens, she will force us to reconsider what reality itself might be.

This is the process I call "re-cognition." Like its counterpart "recognition," this term also is intended to describe both the technique and its effect on us.

By challenging our worldviews and our definitions of reality, Lessing sets up an empirical and dialectical relationship between the text and her readers.[16] Through her narrators, she is forcing us to contend with information that is incompatible with the ordinary reality we are aware of experiencing on a daily basis. Yet she has placed this alien information in a setting that is familiar enough for us to recognize the world of her text as fundamentally our own—no matter how strange or alien it might appear to be. We are left then with the dilemma of how much to believe and how much to discount in what we have read. The process we go through in trying to resolve this dilemma I have called re-cognition, because what we are doing as we read her text is rethinking our definitions of what is real, what is possible. It is a term especially suited to describe what goes on in our minds because its occurrence ultimately depends on whether or not we can *recognize* ourselves and our world in her text. For the conflict to take place, we must be able simultaneously to see a familiar and an alien world in her text. It is this very conflict between what we already believe and what she asks us to believe that is at the heart of her science fiction. It is in the dialectical relationship itself (the dialogue) between reader and text that she is able to help us outgrow our narrow concepts of what it means to be human. So, once more, in re-cognition, as in recognition, there is a give and take between text and reader.

In other words, as occurs when we hear a Sufi teaching story—a genre that has influenced much of Lessing's writings—we learn here through the empirical act of reading itself a new way of knowing. Given this as our premise, it is possible to examine the double, and not always overlapping, intentions of Lessing's narrators and those of Lessing herself. To tell their story successfully, Lessing's narrators try to engage our imaginative complicity in their tale. They want us to believe what they are reporting. Lessing, on the other hand, has less vested interest in whether or not we believe the story. What she is more interested in is the dialectical relationship between text and reader. Because she is primarily intent upon shattering our paradigms, it is not the story itself but the telling of the story that she values. Unlike her narrators, Lessing is less concerned with convincing us of an alien reality than she is in subverting our current reality. It is a subtle but crucial difference, as what she intends is not that we believe in another world but that we learn to see this one differently.

Although the formal intentions of Lessing and her narrators do not coincide, their values and perspectives often do. It is through her narrators, for example, that Lessing conveys her ideas about the dangers of aggressive individualism and nationalism and, conversely, the importance of feeling at one with the natural world and other human beings. It is also through her narrators that she draws her readers into the text and subverts our definitions of reality. For the dialectical relationship to arise, it is imperative, after all, that Lessing's narrators validate the existence of other dimensions and persuade us to believe in them, if only imaginatively.

To lend credence to these imaginary alien worlds, Lessing makes particular use of the romantic convention of the guide-leader or mediator, what she calls an envoy. That is, her science fiction is narrated by a figure not unlike Dante's Vergil, someone who can translate—by virtue of special skills, knowledge, or perspective—the meaning of an alien world into recognizable terms. Where Dante's Vergil and Beatrice guide the hero of *The Divine Comedy* through hell, purgatory, and heaven to the ultimate vision of God, Lessing's envoys lead her readers through the bewildering perplexities of other worlds to an awareness of their full human potential. In other words, the narrators in her science fiction provide readers with a stable and fully constituted system of beliefs in terms of which they make sense of the world she describes. In our acceptance of this worldview—however provisional it might be—Lessing establishes the psychological framework by which she convinces us not of the existence of another world but, more central to her purpose, of the validity of her *ideas.*

To achieve the textual recognition on which our re-cognition is based, Lessing uses various other narrative techniques. In *Briefing for a Descent into Hell*, for example, she uses the perspective of a purported madman to bring the shortcomings of our world into focus. These shortcomings become even more evident when Lessing juxtaposes Charles Watkins's inspired narration to the sterile, jargon-filled reports of the medical doctors who attend him (without ever attending *to* him). Lessing also uses these different points of view to establish the co-existence of two incompatible realities. The salient feature of this novel, in fact, is that of contradictory texts, as what Charles reports is directly refuted by the doctors and other authoritative sources within the novel. It is, I believe, in the process of trying to sort out the novel's reality base that we begin to modify our own concept of reality.

A similar process takes place in *The Memoirs of a Survivor*, in which we try to come to terms with the two worlds of the future it describes. The first problem occurs when we learn that we are reading a history of what amounts to our future. The second problem arises when we try to make sense out of, or come to a logical understanding of, the shape-shifting world behind the wall. And a third problem arises when we learn that not only are we having trouble understanding the text, but the narrator herself is having trouble writing it, because what she has to tell us is so bizarre and elusive. In both these books, in other words, Lessing wants us not only to enjoy the story but also to attend closely to how it is being told. In both cases the narrators are faced with internal doubts as to the explanation for and source of their extraordinary experiences. Charles finally accepts the inevitable and undergoes shock treatments in order to regain his so-called rightful memory, a decision that actually means he loses his access to racial memories and higher truths. And the narrator of *Memoirs*, while ultimately finding refuge in her world behind the wall, confesses throughout her narrative to having difficulties in finding the right words to tell us about what she and we both regard as impossible occurrences—a confession that is significant because it reminds us that it is virtually impossible to see that for which we have no words.

The techniques that Lessing uses in *Canopus in Argos* are equally calculated to get us to attend to the narration of each novel. One technique that appears in all the novels she has published so far in this series is that of having someone narrate the story who is not, technically speaking, a human being and whose perspectives, therefore, are strikingly different from our own. *Shikasta*, *The Sirian Experiments*, *The Making of the Representative for Planet 8*, and *The Sentimental Agents* are all told from the perspective of aliens, who in one way or another are virtually immortal. *The Marriages Between Zones Three, Four, and Five* is told by someone who lives in an area on (or around) earth that we would all be hard pressed to identify—given our current understanding of world geography and physical reality.

Shikasta further defamiliarizes reality and calls attention to its text by presenting a multitude of documents, in a variety of typesettings. *The Marriages Between Zones Three, Four, and Five* defamiliarizes reality by presenting two major differing versions of it and simultaneously calling for a merger (a marriage) of these separate viewpoints. Of additional significance in this novel is the fact that its narrator is an official chronicler and often comments directly on the role of language and literature in determining values and behavior. *The Sirian Experiments* defamiliarizes reality—especially our self-destructive anthropocentric views of the universe—by focusing on how its narrator, Ambien II, learns to shed her own imperfect, provincial point of view and accept the more nearly perfect, galactic view of the Canopeans.

In *The Making of the Representative for Planet 8*, Lessing finally shows her hand and reveals the science behind her science fiction as she tries to modify our worldview by illustrating the principles and implications of quantum mechanics. What Lessing seems most concerned with in this novel is a re-examination of physical reality and the attendant philosophical questions such a re-examination inevitably raises. One question her text raises, as part of the process of re-cognition, is whether or not there is such a phenomenon as individual identity. Another question is what it means to survive, not as an individual but as a species, in a world headed for certain destruction. It is with this question that Lessing most radically challenges our Western ethos, as quite remarkably she is apparently able to take comfort in the fact that the death of millions pales beside the emergence of a new form of knowing—a higher form of being, not dependent for its existence on a corporeal body. Although this seems to be an extraordinary, and perhaps morally questionable, attitude for Lessing to take, it does function quite effectively to call our attention to what we really believe in and what we really value. In its use of modern physics the novel also reminds us of J.B.S. Haldane's famous dictum that the "universe is not only queerer than we suppose, but queerer than we can suppose."[17] But even with its scientific foundation, Lessing is not asking that we literally believe in this alien world—or even in her stunning climax. She is asking us to see alien principles and perspectives as

legitimate alternatives to our own. She is also asking us to enter-
tain the proposition that believing is seeing, that we see what we expect to see.

After the dramatic conclusion to *The Making of the Representative for Planet 8*, *The Sentimental Agents* is something of an
emotional letdown, as Lessing returns in this novel to the political
issues she has already examined in great detail in both *Shikasta* and
The Sirian Experiments. What sets this novel apart from them and
makes it interesting—if also occasionally a bit obvious—is
Lessing's concern with the effects of language and rhetoric on
human behavior and thinking. Although this is a theme that runs
throughout *Canopus in Argos*, it is only in the fifth novel that it
really comes into its own as the primary subject under
consideration. In this novel, Lessing uses her narrator not only as a
guide-leader to alien worlds but as a guide to the ideas she holds
about the relationship between language and reality. As this novel
demonstrates, rhetoric is such a powerful determinant of reality
that it can be used by unscrupulous politicians to create imaginary
but believable worlds of their own devising. But in demonstrating
this, the text functions iconoclastically to destroy the same political
fictions it describes. Ironically, it also destroys itself in the process,
thus freeing us from the tyranny of language altogether.

As we have already seen, Lessing's interest in how different
forms of language can be used to effect good or bad change is not
limited to this novel or even to the series itself.[18] All seven of her
science fiction novels show, for example, how language can be used
by those in power to create social myths that would enslave our
minds. But they also show how language can be used by artists like
Lessing as a tool of intellectual liberation, helping us to transcend
both the authority of the state and the boundaries of known reality.
By reminding us of the power of language, therefore, Lessing's
narrators function as her representatives—exemplifying the role
that she herself is playing as a novelist, which is that of a creative
and perceptive intellect forming itself and the world it inhabits. In
creating these alien worlds, of course, Lessing does not pretend to
be presenting the ultimate view of reality; to do so would be to contradict her own philosophy and narrative intentions. But she is ex-
tending our understanding of the world's infinite richness and
strangeness by spinning out a few beguiling alternatives to what we

today consider reality to be. In short, Lessing's science fiction opens the doors of perception to a fantastic, shape-shifting, and utterly unexpected universe. In so doing, it functions to transform the very world itself.

NOTES

1. For another discussion of how the role of Lessing's characters has changed over the years, see Frederick C. Stern, "The Changing 'Voice' of Lessing's Characters: From Politics to Sci Fi," *World Literature Written in English*, 21, no. 3 (Autumn 1982), 456-67. Working from Georg Lukacs's concept of *Weltanschauung*, Stern argues that the characters in Lessing's earlier fiction are used "to mediate ideas in such a way that the reader can understand how *such* a character might come to *such* conclusions" (463; Stern's emphasis). Her latest fiction, on the other hand, is less concerned with mediation, emphasizing as it does "the self-exploration of character in the privacy of his or her own mind" (465).

2. Doris Lessing, "The Small Personal Voice," in *Declaration*, ed. by Tom Maschler (c. 1957; New York: E. P. Dutton & Co., 1958), 187-201. Subsequent page references appear in the text as "SPV."

3. Sheldon Sacks, "Golden Birds and Dying Generations," *Comparative Literature Studies*, 6, no. 3 (September 1969), 274-91. A subsequent page reference appears in the text.

4. Tom Kitwood, " 'Science' and 'Utopia' in the Marxist Tradition," *Alternative Futures: The Journal of Utopian Studies*, 1, no. 2 (Summer 1978), 37. Although it has not always been feasible to do so, I have tried whenever possible in this work to distinguish between "Marxist" politics and "Marxian" thought or criticism—hoping in my use of the latter term to defuse some of the emotionalism surrounding Marxism and to portray more precisely its influence on Lessing's fiction.

5. Herbert Marcuse, *An Essay on Liberation* (Boston: Beacon Press, 1969), 6. Subsequent page references appear in the text as *Essay*.

6. In discussing this switch with Susan Stamberg, Lessing emphasizes its almost accidental nature, protesting that it was not a "*willed* thing." Instead, she says she "found [herself] off into fantasy." From that point in her writing, she adds, "I went on to the other two nonrealistic books. It wasn't that I said 'now, I found this mode that was what I needed' " ("An Interview with Doris Lessing," *Doris Lessing Newsletter*, 8, no. 2 [Fall 1984], 3; Lessing's emphasis).

7. Herbert Marcuse, *One-Dimensional Man: Studies in the Ideology of Advanced Industrial Society* (Boston: Beacon Press, 1964), xii. Subsequent page references appear in the text as Marcuse.

8. One measure of women's literary alienation in this culture can be seen in the fact that, as late as 1966, Richard K. Barksdale could identify seven different types of anti-heroes in American fiction without mentioning women at all; see his "Alienation and the Anti-Hero in Recent American Fiction," *CLA Journal*, 10, no. 1 (September 1966), 1-10.

9. The desire to restructure both language and thinking lies at the heart of much recent feminist literature, criticism, and critical theory. For an overview of this subject, see the special issue "L'Écriture Féminine," *Contemporary Literature*, 24, no. 2 (Summer 1983).

10. Doris Lessing, "Some Remarks," preface to *Re: Colonised Planet 5, Shikasta* (New York: Alfred A. Knopf, 1979), ix.

11. Doris Lessing, "Preface" to *The Sirian Experiments* (New York: Alfred A. Knopf, 1981), ix.

12. Robert Galbreath, "Ambiguous Apocalypse: Transcendental Versions of the End," in *The End of the World*, ed. Eric S. Rabkin et al. (Carbondale and Edwardsville: Southern Illinois University Press, 1983), 54.

13. Darko Suvin, *Metamorphoses of Science Fiction: On the Poetics and History of a Literary Genre* (New Haven and London: Yale University Press, 1979), 4-11.

14. Victor Shklovsky, "Art as Technique," in *Russian Formalist Criticism: Four Essays*, trans. Lee T. Lemon and Marion J. Reis (Lincoln: University of Nebraska Press, 1965), 3-24. For a brief explanation of Brecht's theories of *Verfremdungseffekt* or "estrangement effect," see Marcuse's *One-Dimensional Man*, 66-70.

15. This dynamic relationship between text and reader is similar to that described by Wolfgang Iser in *The Implied Reader: Patterns of Communication in Prose Fiction from Bunyan to Beckett*, especially chapter 11, "The Reading Process: A Phenomenological Approach" (Baltimore and London: The Johns Hopkins University Press, 1974), 274-94.

16. In referring to this dialectical exchange, I have in mind what Stanley Fish describes as a dialectical text in *Self-Consuming Artifacts: The Experience of Seventeenth-Century Literature* (1972; rpt. Berkeley: University of California Press, 1974). In chapter 1, "The Aesthetic of the Good Physician," he describes a "dialectical presentation [as] disturbing, for it requires of its readers a searching and rigorous scrutiny of everything they believe in and live by" (1). It is also didactic as it "asks that its readers discover the truth for themselves, and this discovery is often made at the expense not only of a reader's opinions and values, but of his self-esteem. . . . For the end of a dialectical experience is (or should be) nothing less than a *conversion*, not only a changing, but an exchanging of minds" (1-2; Fish's emphasis).

In "Reading Doris Lessing," Judith Stitzel offers her own account of what happens between herself and several of Lessing's texts, concluding that Lessing "does not tell us what to believe; she forces us to examine how" (*College English*, 40, no. 5 [January 1979], 504).

17. Lessing refers to Haldane's 1927 quotation in her preface to *The Sirian Experiments* (vii). Here, after listing the astonishing claims made by modern physics about the nature of the universe, Lessing says of her own series that she doesn't "want to be judged as adding to a confusion of embattled certainties" (vii).

18. Nor is it limited to her science fiction, as is evidenced by what she says in "The Small Personal Voice."

1.

Disturbing the Universe:
Briefing for a Descent into Hell

Although *Briefing for a Descent into Hell* (1971) has elicited little critical attention in the fifteen years since its publication, it does appear to have played a major role in the development of Lessing's narrative technique and authorial vision. In its emphasis on the co-existence of multiple realities, for example, it anticipates both *The Memoirs of a Survivor* and *Canopus in Argos: Archives*. It also introduces Lessing's controversial concept of a universal, teleological imperative (that which she calls the "necessity" in her Canopus series), her metaphor of astral monitors and messengers, and her technique of using narrators as guide-leaders. It is also the first time that Lessing employs what I have called the complementary formal techniques of recognition and re-cognition. But just as *Briefing* anticipates her subsequent science fiction novels, it also reflects her earlier, more conventional novels. It does so through its account of how society responds to a so-called madman and how this "individual conscience" responds to the pressures of "the collective," the same theme that Lessing says is at the heart of *Children of Violence*.[1] In short, *Briefing for a Descent into Hell* is a kind of bridge between the more conventional fiction she wrote at the beginning of her career and the science fiction she is writing today.

Distinguishing between these two kinds of fiction is something Lessing herself has tried to discourage in critics. Evidence for this can be found in her 1973 review of Kurt Vonnegut's *Mother Night*, in which she praised the author for making "nonsense of the little categories, the unnatural divisions into 'real' literature and the rest."[2] That she abhors most forms of labeling, of course, is clear from several other sources, both fictional and discursive.[3] This abhorrence helps to explain the abundance of paradoxes in her own work—a phenomenon that can prove unsettling to her readers who often wonder just what it is they are supposed to believe. A perfect example of her ability to confound her readers takes place in *Briefing for a Descent into Hell* where paradoxes and internal contradictions abound. In fact, she seems to have built this novel on the two major paradoxes that are central to all her work. The first paradox deals with meaning and the second with narrative technique. Because of this complementary relationship, they are practically inseparable. The two are also the subject of "The Small Personal Voice," Lessing's statement of what it means to be a responsible artist committed to the idea of social change.

In this essay, Lessing identifies the two major strains of twentieth-century writing as being the expressions of two equally misguided schools of thought, Marxism and existentialism. Marxist literature she says is exemplified by a "cheerful little tract about economic advance," while its counterpart is exemplified by a "novel or play which one sees or reads with a shudder of horrified pity for all of humanity" ("SPV," 193). In her view, both of these expressions of the human condition are a "betrayal of what a writer should be" ("SPV," 194); that is, both are "aspects of cowardice, both fallings-away from a central vision, the two easy escapes of our time into false innocence" ("SPV," 194). Although existentialism and Marxism might seem to be diametrically opposed philosophies, Lessing quite rightly sees them as being the "opposite sides of the same coin. One sees man as the isolated individual unable to communicate, helpless and solitary; the other as collective man with a collective conscience" ("SPV," 194). Unwilling to accept in full either vision of humanity, Lessing instead argues for a happy medium between these two polarites, "a resting point, a place of decision, hard to reach and precariously balanced. It is a balance which must be continuously tested and reaffirmed" ("SPV," 194). It is the responsibility of the writer to maintain this precarious balance where a single person is seen as both an individual and part of a collective. The point of rest Lessing describes is not stable but is forever adjusting to circumstances. Instead of making "final judgements or absolute statements of value," therefore, it should acknowledge the right of an individual to submit "voluntarily . . . to the collective, but never finally"; it should also acknowledge the right of each person to make "personal and private judgements before every act of submission" ("SPV," 194).

In taking this position Lessing anticipates the major paradoxical issues of her work. The first, as I have already indicated, deals with meaning. Its paradoxical status depends on the counterweights of the individual conscience and the collective or group mind—the conflicting interests of self and society. It raises the question, in other words, of how the "I" reconciles itself and its own personal needs to the demands and higher needs of the "we," asking how (and if) individuality can co-exist with commonality and communality without becoming totally subsumed within them. The second paradox deals with narrative technique and hinges on the relationship between reader and author. Although the emphasis in this paradox is on form rather than content, the questions it raises are virtually identical to the questions raised by the other. The formal paradox asks how the individual reader can maintain autonomy and self-integrity in the face of the overwhelming *author*ity of the text. It asks how the "eye/I" reading the text can avoid the imperatives of the editorial "we." Putting the two paradoxes together, we get questions like the following: how does Lessing, herself a powerful "I" (eye) that has an urgent need to preach "we," do so without totally subverting the will of the individual "I's" (eyes) of her readers. That is, how can Lessing function as that resting point, the eye of the storm, without sucking her readers into the vortex she describes.

Lessing circumvents some of the problem of authorial authority by setting up a dialectical relationship—an intellectual debate—between her readers and her text. To do this she uses the aforementioned techniques of recognition and re-cognition, which challenge our anthropocentric view of the universe. To avoid alienating us altogether with these violations of known reality, Lessing uses the mediation of narrative guide-leaders. It is the role of her narrators, in other words, to introduce us to concepts and points of view that conflict with what we already know and to do so without completely alienating us. This is why I say that her narrators mediate between us and the text; they stand somewhere in the middle, explaining one world to another, representing one position to another. By utilizing her narrators as guide-leaders to strange new worlds, Lessing keeps the debate with her readers alive and her texts open. But even though these narrators represent these worlds to us, their narrative intentions are not always the same as those of Lessing herself. It is their intention to convince us of the reality of their worlds; it is Lessing's to cast doubt on the reality of our world. By thus distinguishing between her own authorial intentions and those of her narrators, Lessing allows us some additional respite from the absolute authority of a text. This openness is nowhere clearer than in her first science fiction novel where she creates sympathy for her narrator even as she casts doubts on his reliability.

The fact that Charles Watkins may be mad raises some interesting questions regarding the form of this novel. Most pertinent to this study is the question of whether or not *Briefing for a Descent into Hell* can properly be regarded as science fiction. Although much of the story reads like science fiction—such as Charles's Adamic experiences in the new world, his acceptance into the hovering Crystal, and the briefing he receives from the gods—the fact cannot be overlooked that these passages are narrated by someone the doctors consider to be insane. To date, the response of most critics to this fact has been to read the novel as psycho-drama and not as science fiction.[4] Their reasons for doing so seem to stem primarily from the book's often-noted resemblance to a clinical documentation of schizophrenia in R. D. Laing's *The Politics of Experience*—a resemblance that Lessing, somewhat disingenuously, insists is merely coincidental.[5] The major problem with disregarding the book's correspondence to science fiction is that to do so reduces its textual complexity. If it is read only as psycho-drama, Charles Watkins's descriptions of his marvelous journey become simply the ramblings of a well-educated and imaginative madman, whose tale follows the patterns common to the accounts of schizophrenic breakdowns. To read the novel as a case study in madness, therefore, is to lose its major tension—that between the conflicting versions of reality that appear here. For example, Charles claims that he spent part of World War II in Yugoslavia, fighting with the partisans; his friend Miles Bovey, on the other hand, claims that Charles never left North Africa. If we deny that the novel is science fiction, both of these mutually contradictory accounts cannot be true. One must be false. And because it is Charles's credibility that is in question, it is only logical to conclude that what he says is nothing more than a manifestation of his madness. By extension, therefore, anything that he says that contradicts reality as we know it can safely be dismissed as imaginative nonsense.[6]

But if the novel is read as science fiction, on the other hand, all accounts of reality in the novel are, theoretically, valid. What Charles describes as having happened to him at sea, on the Brazilian coast, in the Crystal, and at the briefing is as real (fictionally speaking) as what happens when he emerges from his fantastic journey and finds himself in Central Intake Hospital. As an envoy from another world, Charles (like the Canopean agents to follow) would be perfectly capable of experiencing a reality unknown and unknowable to the rest of us time-bound mortals. What he says happened with the partisans in Yugoslavia could be a result of his ability to live another person's life or even two of his own simultaneously. These speculations aside, how he manages to go to Yugoslavia, however, is less important than the fact that he does insist he went. His insistence in this matter suggests that Charles is author of his own reality and that he is unshaken if it does not always coincide with the reality accepted by others.[7] Reading *Briefing for a Descent into Hell* as science fiction, therefore, brings out what Lessing seems to be suggesting about the nature of reality itself—that it is largely a function of language and perception.[8] As our guide-leader, for example, Charles is responsible for translating Lessing's perception of reality into language that makes sense to us. If we see him as mad, we commit the same error in judgment that his doctors do. If we see him as our guide-leader in a science fiction novel, we have access to Lessing's vision of wholeness and, perhaps more important, we can engage in our own dialectic with her representative.

Although Charles Watkins does not narrate the entire novel, it is his point of view that controls the book. And he is very much our guide-leader, assisting us as we thread our way through his convoluted, metaphorical story. I have suggested that one of the purposes of the guide-leader is to mediate between our world and the alien world Lessing creates in her fiction. This is certainly a major responsibility of this narrator who must try to convince us that what he sees and does is reasonable and possible, given the conventions of the form Lessing has chosen for this novel.[9] Roughly one-half of the book is composed of Charles's narration which is periodically interrupted by the traditional voices of reason represented by the medical profession. The effect of this structure is to support the book's claim that the ravings of a so-called madman are more real and meaningful than the scientific explanations of the doctors who insist on contradicting him at every turn.

Convinced that Charles is having a mental breakdown, they fail to listen to him carefully, behaving themselves with almost stupefying literal-mindedness. When Charles claims variously to be Jason, Jonah, and Sinbad, for example, he is obviously speaking metaphorically. But Doctor Y tells him bluntly that he cannot be all of them. Ever reasonable, Charles insists, "We are all sailors"—an assertion the doctor tries to deny by insisting in his turn, "I am not. I'm a doctor in this hospital."[10] Whether we read this book as science fiction or psycho-drama, this scene is clearly a satirical attack on the medical profession. If we read it only as psycho-drama, however, we simply fault the doctors for not realizing that Charles, like other schizophrenics, is speaking in riddles and metaphors. But if we read it as science fiction, we see that Lessing, in this scene in particular, is using a technique familiar to the genre—that of positing an alternative reality against the skepticism of doubting Thomases (often represented by scientists) who represent conventional thinking. Charles is a space voyager, in other words, who finds it impossible to communicate his discoveries to his own world (a difficulty faced by the lead characters in Ian Watson's *Miracle Visitors* [1978] who also run into bureaucratic skepticism).[11] Charles's language in this passage, which his doctors hear only as gibberish, is in fact full of literary and mythological allusions that are arranged both wittily and meaningfully. Lessing uses this exchange between Charles and his doctors to juxtapose two conflicting points of view with the purpose of undermining the traditional voice of authority and championing its challenger. To do this effectively, she must rely on the challenger himself to guide us over the threshold of skepticism that prevents the hospital staff from experiencing her vision of galactic wholeness.[12] In this instance, although it does not hold true throughout the novel, the intentions of Lessing and her narrator do indeed coincide, as both would subvert the credibility of the conventional voices of reason.

With the purpose of gaining our sympathy for this wanderer, Lessing establishes his amiable personality from the start, when we learn from the general remarks on his admittance sheet at Central Intake Hospital that this patient, whose name is unknown at this point, is "Rambling, Confused, and Amenable" (3). Although she may temporarily predispose us to doubt his sanity and veracity, having described him as rambling and confused, his own poetic language soon wins us over to his side, and we begin to consider the authorities remiss for not being able to appreciate his gifts. Once we realize that Charles is voicing the universal patterns of mythic voyages, we realize that it is the police who are "confused" when they persist in their quixotic notion that he might be a yachtsman (4). When he plays word association games and speaks in silly puns, the doctors reply matter-of-factly that what he says is wrong and proceed to knock him out with drugs. But the reader responds more favorably to these puns, such as when he describes being held "safe across the cross not to say furious currents" (6). Or when riding on the back of a porpoise, he says, "There, there, is my true destination and my love, so, purpose, be sure to hold your course" (38). Because we can *see* the meaning of these puns, as the doctors apparently cannot, we are prepared to journey even further into this man's imagination—a journey that takes the form of recognition and re-cognition as, inevitably, he teaches us to see ourselves from an alien perspective.[13] In short, having sided with Charles against the conventional voices of authority, we are more likely to accept his radical narrative as a reasonable one, one that describes an alternate but equally valid view of reality. That is, as we read his story, we gradually learn to distrust the doctors' perceptions of reality, perceptions that outside the novel would be our own.

For Charles, the doctors do not seem terribly real, an interpretation that is reinforced by the fact that they are called simply X, Y, and Z.[14] At one point he even accuses Doctor Y of being a delusion, stating further, "Things aren't what they seem" (13). This statement summarizes a major theme of the novel, as Lessing repeatedly confronts her readers with the unexpected—often in the form of inverted truths where what we would ordinarily regard as imaginary we are asked to accept as real, and vice versa. After it is established that Charles is an amnesiac, for example, he asserts vehemently that the forgotten life the doctor is trying to impose on him is nothing more than a dream (166). Similarly, when Charles is most active in his alternate world, he is perceived by the hospital staff to be sleeping. Later, when he is fighting to wake up, the nurse reports that he "seems to want to go back to sleep" (156). Just as it seems to be established that he wants to wake up, he complains that they will not let him go back to sleep, that he "must sleep again, where *They* are. Awake is asleep" (165; Lessing's emphasis). As these exchanges illustrate, there is more to reality than meets the eye. We know this to be true because we have seen what the hospital staff cannot, that beyond their own world of scientific objectivity is a transcendent, meaningful reality. Because we have shared Charles's visionary experiences, in other words, there is an ironic distance between us and the hospital staff. The effect of this distance is to shift our own expectations until we accept the authority of the narrator and reject the authority of the authorities.

This shift is central to the meaning of the novel and is crucial to the recognition and re-cognition we experience. That it is central to the novel is clear from the exchanges noted above and from the fact that the novel itself is structured on a parallel shift in perspective. The first part of the novel is told almost entirely from Charles's point of view and primarily contains his detailed account of his fantastic journey that begins with a sea voyage and ends with the divine briefing that precedes his birth.[15] The second part of the novel maintains Charles as the central figure, but the point of view is diffused among the perspectives of several other characters, including his wife Felicity, his mistress Constance Mayne, his friends Miles Bovey and Jeremy Thorpe, and a recent acquaintance Rosemary Baines. Charles's own state of mind also changes from the first to the second part. In the first he is absorbed in his journey and immune to outside influences. In the second he has returned from his journey and has become susceptible to the psychological pressures brought to bear on him by the hospital staff and his family. Finally, both sections contain much of the same information about Charles, but the two accounts reflect the differences in perspective between the sections. For example, in the first section Charles describes a group of women and children who encourage him to participate in a bloody orgy as part of his ritual fall from grace. In the second section, we learn from their own letters that these people are from his "real" life, that they are his wife, his children, and his mistress. The perspective may be radically different but, as Betsy Draine has thoroughly documented, the correspondence is not to be missed.[16]

As close as these correspondences are, however, the novel also contains factual discrepancies that are not accounted for by either part. There is, for example, an extra infant at the orgy that seemingly has no existence in Charles's real life. And, although most of the people who are specifically named in part one play a role in Charles's "real" life, not everyone is accounted for. Furthermore, there are the unanswered questions of whether or not Charles was in Yugoslavia during the war, whether or not he ever attended a divine briefing, and whether or not he is a divine messenger—claims he makes that are otherwise unsupported by the text. As I have pointed out, one way to account for these textual contradictions is to assume that Charles is mad and therefore not to be trusted as a source of reliable information. But this interpretation tends to dismiss the central conflict that lies in the novel's competing views of reality. If, on the other hand, we can accept Charles's account as a valid rendition of an alien reality, we can see that a kind of internal or intra-textual recognition is going on, during which we compare what we know already of Charles with what we are learning about him from his friends and family. In this activity, we discover, much to our growing discomfort, that the doctors in many ways speak for us, as they represent the voice of conventional reality in the novel. Just as they question what he says during his monologues, so we do—even as we recognize much of what he is describing.

In his description of his adventures in the Atlantic, for example, we recognize mythic patterns and heroes as well as the scientific theory that life evolved from the sea. In his inviting description of his adventures in the deserted South American city, we recognize our own primal longings for wholeness and the desire to experience a transcendent reality. In his almost despairing account of the war between the apes and rat-dogs and the pollution it causes, we recognize our own behavior and are forced to admit our own culpability. By anthropomorphizing these creatures, Lessing insures that we will see ourselves—and see ourselves anew—in them. Some of what we read we are glad to recognize. And some we are loath to recognize because of what it forces us to admit about ourselves. But, willing or not, when we recognize ourselves in what Charles describes, we submit to the process of re-cognition, as we learn to see and think differently. This process is particularly unsettling to us when Charles describes things we would ordinarily think of as violations of our physical laws, such as when he climbs on the back of a giant bird, flies over the earth, and observes the rapid unfolding of human history or when he enters the floating Crystal and tells us about his friends who inhabit its facets. Although Lessing uses various narrative strategies to help us overcome our resistance to these accounts, she does use the doctors as her own internal devil's advocates who urge us to deny the spiritual truths that Charles represents. But their role is admonitory in an unexpected way. That is, she uses Charles to inform us of what we are missing out on and the doctors to warn us of what we are condemning ourselves to—if we persist in our strictly dualistic definitions of reality.

One explanation for their blindness (besides the narrative purpose it serves) lies in the kind of expectations they have, a situation that makes Charles's role in the story even more important as far as we are concerned. Echoing the findings of perceptual theorists and anthropologists, Charles points out, in explanation of the behavior of his friends on the ship, that "the expectation of a thing must meet with that thing—or, at least, that is, the form in which it must be seen by you" (17).[17] We see what we expect to see, in other words, and completely overlook that which we do not expect. What happens to Charles also illustrates Kenneth Burke's contention that our terministic screens not only reflect reality but also select and deflect it.[18] Because the doctors expect Charles to ramble incoherently, for example, they hear only nonsense. Confined by their own scientific language and points of view, the doctors are blind to his alien gestalt. As a consequence, they are unable to understand that what they hear as isolated, meaningless fragments are actually related elements of a meaningful whole. Trapped by their own fragmentation, they are blind to the world's interrelatedness and unity.[19] In the doctors' defense, however, it must be said that they

are trapped also by circumstances in a situation that would reinforce their preconceived ideas. We, on the other hand, have the advantage of meeting Charles in a novel, a highly symbolic one at
that. Our expectations are therefore quite different from those of
the poor doctors who of course cannot see that they are in a novel.

The point that Lessing is making here about the relationship between language and perception has an analogue in another recent
science fiction novel, Samuel R. Delany's *Babel-17*. In this novel,
Delany has posited a fairly stock situation in the far future where
what he calls the Alliance is under attack by a group of invaders.
But if the situation is stock, the solution is not. For the Alliance can
only be saved by Rydra Wong, a female spaceship captain, poet,
and linguist who, in stopping the Invaders, must learn to speak and
think in Babel-17, their specialized computer language that lacks
the concept of "I" and is, as a result, a deadly efficient linguistic
weapon for fighting a war. Trapped at one point by the Invaders in
a cunning, unfamiliar web (which is an implied pun for being
trapped in a web of words), Rydra is only able to extricate herself
from it by seeing it through the lens of Babel-17, on whose
principles it has been constructed. The moment she thinks in Babel-
17 she easily escapes the web. The Butcher, one of the tools of the
Invaders, has been programmed with Babel-17 to such an extent
that he has lost all knowledge of "I" and "you." As a result he
kills on command with no sense of compassion or guilt. He only re-
gains his humanity after Rydra painstakingly teaches him about
"I" and "you" and then, as in any good romance, falls in love
with him.

But where Delany's novel suggests the importance of "I," Lessing's suggests the danger in it. It is not unimportant to Delany's
book that Rydra Wong is a poet, as she speaks for others in
asserting her self in her writing. Her galactic reputation in fact rests
almost entirely on her ability to read people and then describe their
fears and desires as her own. Coincidentally, both she and Charles
Watkins, in contemplating the significance of what they are doing,
hit upon the same series of perceptual puns—a series also discovered by Kenneth Burke. Referring to her own poems as
"Definitions of 'I' each great and precise," Rydra makes the
qualitative leap to "I / Aye / Eye, the self, a sailor's *yes*, the organ
of visual perception."[20] Charles, trying to navigate in unfamiliar

waters on his mythic voyage, says "The eye that would measure the pace of sand horses, as I watch the rolling gallop of sea horses would be an eye indeed. Aye Aye. I. I could catch a horse, perhaps and ride it, but for me a sea horse, no horse of sand, since my time is man-time and it is God for deserts" (5). The richness of this passage is striking, with its puns spinning out the manifold meanings of "I / eye / aye." The "I" is the center of a changing universe: perceiving it, naming it, knowing it—in short, affirming its existence. But "I" as a single entity is still limited; it is only able to "sea [see] horse." Only the "eye" of God, the triple (multiple, endless) being, can measure the movements of the eternal deserts. Burke, in his essay on Emerson's "Nature," also finds a progression from "I" to "Eye" to "Aye," arguing, much as Lessing's entire novel does, that "transcendence involves dialectical processes whereby something HERE is interpreted *in terms of* something THERE, something *beyond* itself."[21] That is, the I (eye) seeing in terms of a beyond helps to affirm it and thus " 'builds a bridge,' " through language, between two "disparate realms" (Burke, 189).

This is exactly what Charles tries to do after he has renounced his individuality and entered the realm of universality. Once he is absorbed by the Crystal and retraces his history back to the briefing and his subsequent birth as "Charles Watkins," for example, he tries to build a bridge for us by speaking almost entirely in images of wholeness and relatedness. Even the setting he describes reinforces these images, as the Crystal descends on a night with a full moon and appears over a circle in the city square—all archetypal images of a mandala, representing psychological wholeness and integration. Finding his lost friends in the very structure of the Crystal, he says that their "minds lay side by side, fishes in a school, cells in honeycomb, flames in fire, and together we made a whole in such a way that it was not possible to say, Here Charles begins, here John or Miles or Felicity or Constance ends" (106). He also realizes that the mind of man is intertwined with "the animal mind" and describes the relationship as the "locking together of the inner pattern in light with the other world of stone, leaf, flesh, and ordinary light" (107). In his new state of awareness, he is able to see that mankind's great error has been its insistence on individuality: "for saying I, I, I, I, is their madness, this is where they have been struck lunatic, made moon-mad, round the bend, crazy, for these microbes are a whole, they form a unity" (120). When he is born into his human form, he tries to cling to the knowledge that "THE THREE IS ME," but he soon forgets as he is socialized into the Cartesian dualities of Western culture (148).[22]

In his loss of primal memories, Charles is no different from the rest of us who suffer from a kind of racial amnesia, having forgotten that our "mind and flesh and life and movements are made of star stuff, sun stuff, planet stuff" (130). Looking for a way to express the lost unity he has recovered and the cycle of history he has uncovered, our guide-leader, who in "real" life is a classics professor, turns to his own field for metaphors and describes the planets as personifications of mythological figures who are trying to save humanity from its own foolishness. In attendance at the conference on Venus where Charles is briefed are such luminaries as Minna Erve (Minerva), the Light (Jupiter), and Merk Ury (Mercury). According to Charles, when the world has been especially threatened by disintegration, Mercury, the "disseminator of laws from God's singing centre" and "Master of Words," has been sent to earth with a reminder that we are all part of the cosmic whole (117, 134). Like the envoys who appear on earth in *Canopus in Argos*, it is implied that in this role of messenger he has been variously Jesus, Mohammed, and Buddha. In each case, the message that had begun as so-called planetary impulses has been translated into words for transmission. The gods have been forced to operate this way, according to Charles, because " 'I gotta use words when I talk to you' " (123). (This, of course, is a line from T. S. Eliot's "Sweeney Agonistes.") Theorizing that the planets have tried to warn earth of impending disaster at several points in its history, Charles suggests that these messages would have had to be delivered in person because "They have to use words when they talk to us" (126). Later, he tells the doctors that he was at a briefing with "God I think . . . I gotta use words. But if not God, what" (162). When the doctor accuses him of claiming to be a god, Charles remembers enough of his message to tell him, "You as well," implying that we are all gods (162). He also remembers the truth that god is light (probably in part because this is also a standard Christian image), as even during his darkest moments he has been able to see a small flicker of light in Doctor Y, whom he rather trusts. But he is able to see no light at all in

Doctor X, who apparently as an unknown is well named and who is disliked intensely by Charles, for good reason: it is Doctor X who finally orders shock treatments for him. But beyond these few details of the briefing, Charles has completely forgotten his message—and his previous life.

But what he has done, if not for the doctors at least for us, is to make permanent his message in the form of literature which he defines as "that sequence of words, I've got to use words" (123). He has, therefore, in effect made one his message and the novel.[23] In so doing, he functions in many respects as the voice of Lessing herself, reminding us of what our true relationship to the world has been, what it should be, and through his own personal tragedy where it has gone wrong. In transmitting this message, it is not unimportant that Lessing has chosen a madman as her spokesman. This decision suggests that she herself might have been uncertain about how this message would be received by her readers. Her doubts and pessimism on this subject are seemingly reinforced by the conclusion when Charles's godlike memory and perspective are wiped out by the electroshock treatments he receives. But all is not lost. For, although it is true that the messenger has been silenced, the message has been safely delivered.

The fact that the message has been safely delivered, irrespective of the narrator's fate, suggests that there was more to Lessing's choice of a purported madman as narrator than any doubts she might have had about her own persuasiveness. For one thing, it is not uncommon in contemporary literature for mental institutions and the mentally ill to function as metaphors of the modern world, as occurs in Ken Kesey's *One Flew Over the Cuckoo's Nest* and Marge Piercy's *Woman on the Edge of Time*. In a more venerable tradition, Charles is also an example of the wise fool, whose observations about life challenge our certainty and complacency by forcing us to recognize ourselves in unsettling images. Finally, descriptions of madness are not unknown in the rest of Lessing's fiction, as is apparent in both *The Golden Notebook* and *The Four-Gated City*. Throughout her fiction Lessing seems to use the metaphor of madness to express her ideas about the relationship among language, perception, and reality. On the question of Charles's sanity, I really doubt that she cares—as he himself of course would care—whether or not we believe his wild tales of wandering on the Atlantic ocean or the plains of South America. Instead, I think she cares more about what his narration does to our minds. This is the point where their intentions diverge. Charles, in reciting his story, is trying to provide his audience (both the doctors and us) with a graphic, truthful account of what he has experienced as an astral messenger. Lessing, on the other hand, uses the conflict between what Charles asserts and what we believe to unsettle our views of reality—a conflict, as I have argued, that is reinforced by the conflict between Charles and his doctors.

Even though she does not care what we believe, she still creates a situation where the participants care. By maintaining these conflicts throughout the novel (until at last Charles is worn down by them and agrees to shock treatment), therefore, Lessing continually pushes us to take sides in the matter of who is right and who is wrong here. And by not giving us enough information to make a final decision, she raises the question of what reality is and from where it comes. For in this novel there is no one reality, there are only realities—one perhaps more familiar than the other but both equally valid textually speaking (an observation that can be made equally well about multiple realities of *The Golden Notebook*, a novel that preceded *Briefing* by nine years). I do not think that Lessing wants to convince us that Charles's experiences are literally real. I do think she wants to help us explore the unknown territory of our minds. It is therefore not the reality of the text she wants us to experience but the reality of reading the text. It is the process itself, our intellectual and imaginative engagement with the dialectic, that she is interested in. Through this dialectical exchange she challenges us to join Charles in his miraculous journey to points unknown. If we accept the challenge, we too will experience the awful joys and madness of transcendence. We too will dare to disturb the universe.

NOTES

1. Doris Lessing, "The Small Personal Voice," in *Declaration*, ed. by Tom Maschler (c. 1957; New York: E. P. Dutton & Co., 1958), 196. Subsequent page references appear in the text as "SPV."

2. Doris Lessing, "Vonnegut's Responsibility," *New York Times Book Review*, 4 February 1973, p. 35.

3. Lessing's most famous attack on the urge to divide and label occurs, of course, in *The Golden Notebook* and her 1971 preface to it (1962; rpt. New York: Bantam, 1973).

4. For discussions of *Briefing for a Descent into Hell* as an example of a fictionalized schizophrenic journey, see: Lois A. Marchino, "The Search for Self in the Novels of Doris Lessing," *Studies in the Novel*, 4, no. 2 (Summer 1972), 252-61; Marion Vlastos, "Doris Lessing and R. D. Laing: Psychopolitics and Prophecy," *PMLA*, 91, no. 2 (March 1976), 245-58; Roberta Rubenstein, "Briefing on Inner Space: Doris Lessing and R. D. Laing," *Psychoanalytic Review*, 63, no. 1 (Spring 1976), 83-93, and "*Briefing for a Descent into Hell*," chapter 7 of her *The Novelistic Vision of Doris Lessing: Breaking the Forms of Consciousness* (Urbana: University of Illinois Press, 1979), 175-99.

5. In *The Novelistic Vision of Doris Lessing*, Rubenstein quotes from a letter she received from Lessing to the effect that she had not read Laing's book and, in fact, had taken the name of Watkins, which is the same surname that Laing uses, "out of the telephone book" (From Letter to Roberta Rubenstein dated 17 November 1972), 197.

6. Or we can agree with Douglas Bolling that Charles's "psychic energies transform the literal into the imaginative truth of art" ("Structure and Theme in *Briefing for a Descent into Hell*," *Contemporary Literature*, 14, no. 4 [Autumn 1973], 563). Reading Charles's account as "art," however, avoids the question of whether or not he literally experienced what he claims to have.

7. Robert S. Ryf puts it well in "Beyond Ideology: Doris Lessing's Mature Vision," where he states that there is in this novel, as in *The Golden Notebook* and *The Four-Gated City*, "a recognition of the primacy of experience itself over attempts to categorize it, a conviction that abstractions ultimately give way to the on-going and inscrutable processes of life itself" (*Modern Fiction Studies*, 21, no. 2 [Summer 1975], 201). Similarly, Roberta Rubenstein, in "Outer Space, Inner Space: Doris Lessing's Metaphor of Science Fiction," finds that "the important focus is the unique mind, asserting its own primary reality over the forces which would distort and destroy it" (*World Literature Written in English*, 14, no. 1 [April 1975], 196).

8. To read this novel as science fiction is not to neglect or deny the influence of Laing; see, for example, Douglas Bolling, "Structure and Theme in *Briefing for a Descent into Hell*" (cited above). Lessing herself refers to her novel on the frontispiece of the hardcover edition as "Category: Inner-Space Fiction—For there is never anywhere to go but in" (New York: Alfred A. Knopf, 1971).

9. In "Structuring the Reader's Response: *Briefing for a Descent into Hell*," Guido Kums discusses the "methods by which the reader is brought to change his loyalties, i.e., to reject values which he has so far accepted, and to accept values which seem strange and unfamiliar" (*Dutch Quarterly Review of Anglo-American Letters*, 11, no. 3 [1981], 197). The methods he describes are those of " 'naturalization' (or 'recuperation') of a strange fantasy world" and the "alienation effect" on our everyday world (197, 203). Lessing's success in naturalization is such that Kums calls her novel "a new myth for our time" (208).

10. Doris Lessing, *Briefing for a Descent into Hell* (New York: Alfred A. Knopf, 1971), 8. Subsequent page references appear in the text.

11. In "A Briefing for *Briefing*: Charles Williams' *Descent into Hell* and Doris Lessing's *Briefing for a Descent into Hell*," Ellen Cronan Rose calls Charles's "adventures a psychic quest [that] takes place at the hallucinatory level as an actual voyage, at the psychological as a return to primal images and myths, among them the myth of Eden" (*Mythlore*, 4, no. 1 [September 1976], 11).

12. I am using "threshold" here in the way defined by Mircea Eliade, in *The Sacred and the Profane: The Nature of Religion*, where he calls it "the limit, the boundary, the frontier that distinguishes and opposes two worlds—and at the same time the paradoxical place where those worlds communicate, where passage from the profane to the sacred world becomes possible" (trans. Willard R. Trask [New York: A Harvest Book, Harcourt, Brace & World, 1959], 27).

13. Robert Ryf interprets these passages, which he claims are "ostensibly a part of [Charles's] derangement," as more precisely functioning "to suggest meanings beyond the discursive" ("Beyond Ideology," 197).

14. The fact that they are named simply X, Y, and Z also suggests their scientific detachment. It also quite possibly suggests that their sympathies lie with scientific positivism, which has as its major goal the absolute identification of object and term.

15. In the Knopf edition this runs from page 3 to 148.

16. Betsy Draine, *Substance Under Pressure: Artistic Coherence and Evolving Form in the Novels of Doris Lessing* (Madison: University of Wisconsin Press, 1983). See chapter 5, "*Briefing for a Descent into Hell*: Composition by Correspondence," 89-110.

17. In *The Crack in the Cosmic Egg: Challenging Constructs of Mind and Reality*, for example, Joseph Chilton Pearce says that "our concepts, our notions or basic assumptions, *actively direct* our percepts" and, further, that "our inherited representation, our world view, is a language-made affair" ([New York: Pocket Books, 1973], 2, 4; Pearce's emphasis). He

bases his own conclusions on the studies and theories of Claude Levi-Strauss, Jerome Bruner, Susanne K. Langer, Benjamin Lee Whorf, and Alfred North Whitehead.

18. Kenneth Burke, "Terministic Screens," chapter 3 in his *Language as Symbolic Action: Essays on Life, Literature and Method* (1966; rpt. Berkeley: University of California Press, 1973), 44-62.

19. For a physicist's view of fragmentation and wholeness, see David Bohm, *Wholeness and the Implicate Order* (London, Boston and Henley [England]: Routledge & Kegan Paul, 1981).

20. Samuel R. Delany, *Babel-17* (New York: Ace Books, 1966). 145.

21. Kenneth Burke, "I, Eye, Ay—Concerning Emerson's Early Essay on 'Nature,' and the Machinery of Transcendence," in his *Language as Symbolic Action* (cited above), 200.

22. Robert Ryf suggests a complementary idea when he says that the "world of ideology and structure is an either/or world; Charles, however, inhabits, at least in part, a both/and world, a realm of existence free from the strictures of closed systems. Language is such a system; if not completely closed, at least relatively so" ("Beyond Ideology," 198).

23. As Ellen Cronan Rose observes, by a "perverse process, *words* come to define reality. How is the patient Charles Watkins to know which is real life, which his fantasy? 'You'll have to *take my word for it*, I'm afraid,' the doctor tells him" ("A Briefing," 12; my emphasis).

2.

Through the Walls of Convention: *The Memoirs of a Survivor*

In *The Memoirs of a Survivor* (1974) Lessing's readers experience a cognitive change similar to the one that takes place in *Briefing for a Descent into Hell*. Although both novels utilize the same narrative techniques of recognition and re-cognition, the intellectual problems they pose are not the same. In *Briefing*, as we have seen, Lessing modifies our view of reality by providing us with a narrator whose bizarre but compelling visions engage us in a dialectical confrontation as we try to work out whether or not Charles Watkins is really insane. In *Memoirs*, on the other hand, she modifies our view of reality by asking us to imagine the existence of another dimension—a world just on the other side of a wall, a quite ordinary wall in an apartment complex. What Lessing establishes as the problem of this novel, therefore, is not the question of whether or not we can trust the narrator but the question of whether or not we can accept the world behind the wall. In setting up this problem, once more she confronts us with extensive defamiliarization that disturbs our view of reality itself. Once more she engages us in an inevitable process of change simply by the fact that we are reading her novel and attempting to solve its mysteries and resolve its paradoxes.

Like all of her science fiction, *The Memoirs of a Survivor* is narrated by someone who acts as our guide-leader, introducing us to these mysteries and helping to explain them. Because these narrators represent Lessing herself, it is surely significant, as I discussed above, that the narrator of her first science fiction novel is someone the authorities regard as insane. It is also significant that the narrator of *Memoirs* is someone whose personal testimony conflicts with official accounts of what happened at the time of her writing, suggesting that Lessing continues to see her role as an advocate of the people and a challenger of the state. It is also noteworthy in this context that the narrator of *Memoirs*, whom I shall call the Survivor, never reveals her name and almost accidentally lets it slip that she is a woman.[1] In fact, what this woman has to say about her own life is remarkably little, considering her central role in the novel. It is as though her identity were less important than her function as narrator. In the larger context of Lessing's science fiction, we can see that the Survivor's relative anonymity is part of a pattern, whereby the individual identities of her narrators become almost inconsequential in light of their roles as mediators, envoys, and witnesses. In their roles as guide-leaders, Lessing's narrators evolve toward the concept of an ideal author who is virtually an ego-less representative of all humanity. In *Briefing*, for example, although the narrator is named and has a personal history, he regards himself as Everyman and a divine messenger of cosmic wholeness. In the first three books of *Canopus in Argos*, the narrators also speak for humanity, until finally, in the character of Doeg in *The Making of the Representative for Planet 8*, the narrator is absolutely identified with his role as spokesman—apparently merging his role as representative and memorialist.[2] Thus it fits a pattern when the narrator of *Memoirs* is primarily important because of her role as witness and memorialist. It is a sign that, although Lessing may be decreasing her emphasis on the personal identity of her narrators, she is increasing their importance as our narrative representatives.

Complicating this novel, as happens in Lessing's other science fiction, is the fact that her narrator is simultaneously addressing two audiences. Obviously, all her narrators, by definition, are addressing us. At the same time, however, these narrators also address audiences within the text. That is, Charles Watkins is speaking—whether consciously or unconsciously—to the medical personnel who are attending him in the hospital. The Survivor also addresses an implied story audience that has apparently shared the experiences she is about to relate. The first sentence establishes her double audience as she declares, "We all remember that time" (3). The identity of this "We" remains uncertain, however, as the time referred to in the novel is in our future. This ambiguity suggests that just as the Survivor is a kind of universal author, her readers constitute a kind of universal audience, who co-exist in and out of the text and in and out of time.

Like most of Lessing's other narrators, the Survivor is quite self-conscious in her work, openly stating that she is writing a "history" which she hopes will be "truthful" (108).[3] Although it should help that her audience remembers "that time," she still has trouble putting this common history into words, implying, through this admission, that somehow the language is incapable of expressing the reality of "that time." The problem is serious enough that she opens her memoirs with a disquisition on the difference between experiencing events and later trying to record them, a difference not unknown to Anna Wulf who ponders its consequences in *The Golden Notebook*.[4] In her account, the Survivor notes that the act of looking back necessarily brings to light things that had gone unnoticed when they first happened. Of the fact that she saw whales and dolphins that were "coloured scarlet and green," for example, she says that she "did not understand at the time what it was [she] was seeing" (4). In part she does not know what she is seeing because she has never seen red and green whales before, and it is virtually impossible to see things that are unknown or have no precedent. This is true because what we are able to see at a given time is largely determined by what we expect to see, which in turn is determined both by what we have seen before and by the language we use.[5] And in part she doubts what she sees because it was not "official" or "respectable" (4). In short, she has trouble writing her memoirs because there is no common language available to describe the unprecedented and bizarre events of the time.

The trouble the narrator has in writing her memoirs has a textual analogue in June Ryan, the lower-class girl who moves into the narrator's flat. June comes of a class of people the narrator describes as being the "despair of the authorities long before the collapse of the old society" (117). The parents were uneducated and often drunk—as were their eleven children. Their house was "filthy, and what furniture it had fit for a rubbish dump" (120). Occasionally one of them would get a job, but more frequently they lived off welfare and petty theft. In sum, "they had opted out; it was all too much for them" (122). The narrator attributes the Ryans's failure to their impoverished verbal skills. June's poverty of language is so severe, in fact, that the narrator can barely understand her. She blames this on the fact that the educated class has never found a way of teaching verbal skills to the lower class, that it has instead "excluded" people like June and her family "from all that richness" (110). Fittingly, once society breaks down, the Ryans flourish. For the most part they do far better than those middle-class people "who either lived on pretending that nothing was *really* happening" or dropped out altogether because they could not "bear an existence where respectability and gain could no longer measure the worth of a person" (123; Lessing's emphasis).

In situations such as the Survivor describes, where the division between language and reality has become too wide to ignore, only those who can adapt to the new reality can survive. This adaptation is made easier—and can in many cases be said to be dependent on—the availability of a language system that reflects the new reality. This situation is as true of scientific revolutions as it is of social upheavals.[6] When the world has been shown, either through scientific experiment or shared experience, to be markedly different from what we once thought it was, we must have a language to describe it; failing this we will neither be able to inhabit it comfortably or bend it to our will. As Lessing is all too aware, the language we use determines how we perceive the world, just as the world helps to determine our language. But what we tend to forget, and what Lessing's fiction reminds us, is that our language systems are artificial constructions that give us only an approximation of reality, not a replica of it.[7]

Although, as Lessing's writing attests, language can indeed be revolutionary, it tends more often to protect and perpetuate the status quo. In this role it acts as a blind, hiding us from what is really going on. This function of language, I would argue, is central to what Lessing is trying to convey in *The Memoirs of a Survivor*. Here the world of everyday reality is represented by a city in the advanced stages of decay, where nothing works any longer except the self-serving bureaucratic machinery that feeds off the weaknesses of the people. As things fall apart, the authorities try to camouflage the disaster by putting out official bulletins that have nothing at all to do with the reality of the situation—using language, in short, to obscure the crisis the city faces. This is the same kind of double-speak satirized by George Orwell in *1984.*

Aware of the propensity of language to deflect reality, Lessing is also aware of its ability to reflect it or even sometimes create it. Thus, although she is surely warning us to mend our ways, she does not leave us entirely without hope. Hope comes in the alternatives to chaos that appear in her description of the world behind the wall. In these passages Lessing, like other utopian writers, is trying to make it easier for us to realize another way of life by giving it form through language (for more on this, see the introduction above). Because much of what she would have us see and do has no precedent in everyday life, in inventing a new world, she has taken on the difficult task of inventing a new language to describe it. She is not giving us a new grammar or a new vocabulary, as many feminist utopian writers have tried recently. But she is giving us new images and new metaphors, the effect of which is to transform our view of reality. She is giving us one of the essential tools that we will need to build a new world when we finally accept the fact that we can no longer live in this one.

The narrative techniques that she uses in this novel, as I have already mentioned, are those of narrative guide-leader, recognition, and re-cognition. Our need for a guide-leader is especially acute here because there are two different kinds of reality in this book, each one represented by a different physical setting and each one inviting our recognition. There is the world of the streets, where civilization is rapidly consuming itself through its own excesses. This is the future we can perhaps literally look forward to if we believe the doomsday scenarios of contemporary demographers. There is also the world behind the wall, which the narrator periodically visits and which, even in its worst manifestations, holds out more hope than the world of the streets. Stationed between them and functioning almost as a neutral zone or an airlock is the flat itself where the narrator lives with two companions—a young girl named Emily Cartright and Emily's pet, a creature named Hugo which is half dog and half cat.

More of an observer than a participant, the narrator is our window to the futuristic world that Lessing has imagined in this book. The role she plays in the story is that of guardian to Emily, who, after she is delivered to the narrator by a mysterious stranger, becomes the heroine (the new Eve) of the story. As Emily ventures into the dangerous world of youth gangs that terrorize the city (which is not identified but which is no doubt London), she provides the narrator with firsthand information about the decline of civilization and the emergence of new social units.[8] The narrator records and interprets this information, trying to give form and meaning to a world being torn apart from within. While Emily provides her with knowledge of the outside world, the narrator provides us with knowledge of the inner world she finds behind the wall of her flat. In effect, she stands between the phenomenal world of the streets and the ideal or mental (but equally real) world behind the wall, mediating between them as she writes her memoirs.[9]

Not only does the narrator mediate between two levels of reality in the text, she also mediates between us and the text itself. It is her responsibility as guide-leader to explain these worlds to us and to describe them with enough conviction for us to experience both rec- ognition and re-cognition. Her role is critical in establishing the normative vision of the novel because both worlds are foreign to our own and yet both are designed to invite our recognition. The world she describes outside the flat exists in the future, but it also has the bleak and frightening familiarity of what we recognize today as the worst of urban life. (The world of the flat takes place in the same future time but focuses less on the public hell of the streets and more on the private limbo of an individual citizen trapped between possibilities.) The world the narrator encounters behind the wall is a fantastic shape-shifting one, composed of events that do not and can not occur in the reality we normally experience. And yet it too we recognize, as it has the haunting famil- iarity of our dreams and imaginative literature. In short, like most science fiction, this novel contains both the foreign and the familiar. Because Lessing wants us to recognize that our current wasteful be- havior will bear fruit in the chaos and corruption of her future world, it is crucial that this world bear some resemblance to our own.[10] It is the narrator's responsibility to see to it that we do make this connection, just as it is her responsibility to help us over the threshold of doubt into an alternative world that lies on the other side of conventional thinking. Only here can we escape the impending catastrophe and recover our ability to live in harmony with nature and one another. To help us make this journey, the narrator must convince us of what she calls "the ordinariness of the extraordinary" (18).

Looking back on what is our future, she characterizes the time when things finally fell apart as being marked by "the combination of the bizarre, the hectic, the frightening, the threatening . . . with what was customary, ordinary, even decent" (18-19). (Oddly, this sounds almost like a definition of science fiction itself, as it balances the bizarre with the customary and ordinary, using the former to comment on the latter.) Perhaps the best example of this schizoid situation occurs near the end of the novel when the youth gangs have themselves lost their cohesiveness, and children as young as four and five murder adults in order to eat them. One group of these feral children lives in the same building as the narrator and is, as she soon learns, quite capable of killing her and Emily simply "because we were their friends. They knew us" (205). After trying to break into the flat to murder them, the "next day some of the children . . . came down to us and we spent a pleasant time together . . ." (206; Lessing's ellipses). If we are shocked and repulsed by the children's actions, the narrator is not. For in her world, this kind of behavior is common enough, and she struggles to "convey the normality of it, the ordinariness of sitting there . . . and thinking, Well, well, it might have been you who planned to stick a knife into me last night" (206). Like similar scenes in more naturalistic literature, this one generates horror in us partly by its content and partly because it is reported without evident emotion. By understating how truly awful things are, the narrator manages to communicate how truly representative of her era this event is.

By accumulating similar evidence that would repulse us, the narrator gradually shuts off all avenues of escape except one, that being the world behind the wall. In this world of the future that Lessing has imagined—this world that so resembles our own—the traditional comforts and havens have turned deadly. Except for that of a few hardy bureaucrats like the Whites, family life has all but disappeared, and children, as we have seen, roam the streets like packs of wild animals. Friendship and acquaintance, rather than being examples of mutual love and support, are virtually meaningless relationships and are often, as in the case of the children trying to break into the narrator's flat, excuses for attack and abuse. The home is no longer safe, either from outside attack or the pollutants that hang in the air. Even the countryside, that last refuge of the imperiled imagination, is never confirmed to be safe from the urban plague. Although great caravans have sought refuge from terror and starvation by fleeing to the countryside, no one returns to tell whether or not life is better there. Our own feelings of claustrophobia, which are the cumulative effects of reading about these horrors, finally impel us to seek refuge with the narrator in the world behind the wall. The world of the future is so bleak and ultimately terrifying that we gratefully accept an alternative to it, even if this alternative violates our conventional concepts of physical reality.

At the same time that the outside world predisposes us to escape into another dimension, the alternative world itself has become inviting on its own terms.[11] It has become inviting, in part, because the narrator has managed to convince us that, contrary to our doubts, it could (if it does not already) exist. One way she overcomes our initial skepticism is by acknowledging that she shares it. When she introduces us to the fact that there are inhabited rooms behind the wall of her flat, for example, she tells us that what she "was hearing was impossible," because, structurally speaking, a corridor is on the other side of that wall, not another world (8). Although what she hears is impossible and therefore also potentially frightening, she is reassured by the strictly "ordinary" sounds that come from behind the wall (12). In short, just as she does with the world outside the flat, in her description of this other dimension, the narrator stresses the ordinariness of the extraordinary. In stressing the ordinariness of these events, she is, in Jonathan Culler's terms, attempting to "naturalize" the text—something most of Lessing's narrators do in one way or another (see chapter 5 below).[12] Once she slips through the wall, for example, she says that "this place held what I needed, knew was there, had been waiting for—oh, yes all my life. . . . I *knew* this place, *recognised* it" (13; my emphases). Just as we recognize in her future world aspects of our own world, she recognizes in her new world aspects of her old one. Not only is the experience of visiting another dimension nothing to fear, but it is pleasantly familiar and potentially gratifying to the narrator.

As suggested by the words "knew" and "recognised," the narrator has known tacitly about "that other life" long before she "*realised* what it was" (7; Lessing's emphasis). But even though this place is familiar to her, she still has trouble believing that it exists. Because of her doubts she keeps forgetting about it. Only after several visits is she finally able to retain a "consciousness of that other life" (7). The transformation of her subconscious knowledge into conscious knowledge, she says, can be described "in the word 'realise,' with its connotation of a gradual opening into comprehension" (7). This process of recovering hidden knowledge appears elsewhere in Lessing's fiction (see, for example, chapter 6 below) and suggests the influence of Sufism on her writing, as the Sufis, according to Nancy Shields Hardin, believe that "to forget 'is the way of men.' "[13] But "to realise" also means to make real. Thus her newfound ability implies that in consciously remembering "that other life" she has somehow helped to make it real, just as her description of it helps to make it real to us.

The world behind the wall basically constitutes a "promise" of a better life—a promise that did not fail her, "no matter how difficult things became later" (14). Although the narrator says that "it was always a liberation to step away from [her] 'real' life into this other place, so full of possibilities, of alternatives," it does have its unpleasant aspects (64). This is because what happens in the alternate world is somehow connected to what happens in the outside world.[14] What disturbs the narrator most are those times from Emily's childhood she is forced to witness. It is during these visits that the narrator learns to see the world as Emily once saw it, a perspective she needs to have in order to help Emily in the real world. She labels these visits her "personal" experiences and characterizes them as an emotional prison (41). Less confining are her impersonal visits, when she does not run into anyone she knows. But there is one particularly bad time when she experiences a "lowered vitality, a sense of foreboding, instead of the lively and loving anticipation" she had felt at first (64). During this time, which takes place right after Emily has joined a gang on the street, the narrator tells us, by "inheriting this extension of my ordinary life, I had been handed, again, a task. Which I was not able to carry through" (63). The task, cleaning house, is a metaphor for what she must do psychologically if she is to prepare herself and Emily for permanent residence in the world behind the wall. As our guide-leader and mentor, she must also prepare us for this moment, when she, Emily, and others enter a luminous vision of wholeness—a task that involves convincing us of its reality.[15]

This is no easy task because the very quality of the world behind the wall that makes it recognizable to us is the same one that makes it hard for us to believe in. When the narrator describes the shape-shifting, elusive world behind the wall, for example, it is inevitably our dreamworld that we think of, a correlation that gives us a sense of place we can recognize, albeit a disturbing one. In this strange world of the novel we also recognize fairly common events, such as the growing pains of a young child and the tensions simmering be-tween her parents, but even these scenes shift about with little re-gard for logic. Thus they too reinforce our sense of having entered a dreamworld. This similarity to what we experience in a dream is reinforced in still other scenes where the narrator is assigned to cer-tain tasks that have little resemblance to real life. For example, at one point she joins a group of people who are placing colored frag-ments of material on a carpet to bring its pattern back to life; even more strangely, when she looks back after she leaves, the room it-self has simply disappeared—something we might expect to occur in a dream. But even though the events of this alien world are re-lated to our dreamworld, they are not, as the narrator makes per-fectly clear, to be relegated to this world.

In trying to convince us that this other world is indeed real, she in-sists that the people she sees in the personal scenes are real (her word) and not "forces or presences" (66). The point she makes in claiming that these people are real is significant because of her neg-ative attitudes toward them. If she so dreads encountering them, as she apparently does, she could alleviate some of her dread by claiming they are illusions or otherwise unreal. But because she stresses the fact that they are real, she lends support to the interpre-tation that so is the world they inhabit. The narrator also helps to affirm the reality of this other world by referring to her life outside as her "ordinary life," implying that she has both an ordinary and an extraordinary one (100). Furthermore, she calls into question the reality of this ordinary life by referring to it as her " 'real' life," using the inverted commas to imply that it is not real at all (64).

Although she continues to distinguish between the two worlds throughout her narrative, eventually she describes the invasion of the outer world by the inner one. Her purpose in distinguishing between them, therefore, seems to have been a strategy to establish the validity of both, so that when they begin to take on each other's qualities, it is clear that one is not more real than the other. When she is behind the wall, for example, she says that "the ordinary logical time-dominated world of everyday did not exist" (145). And, conversely, when she is in her " 'ordinary' life" [*sic*], she forgets, "sometimes for days at a time, that the wall could open, has opened, would open again" (145). Even though the two are different, they do begin to share certain qualities as things become increasingly desperate on the outside. In comparison to the recent past, for example, the narrator finds that the present is "remarkable and dreamlike" (126). Moreover, as the final summer draws to a close, "there was as bad a state of affairs in the space behind the wall as on this side, with us" (155). The narrator characterizes this state as being one of reduced possibilities, claustrophobia, and disorder (156). Of this situation she also remarks that perhaps it had always been so, that perhaps she was simply seeing the alien world more clearly than she had been able to before.

Whether she is seeing it more clearly or whether it has always been more similar to the outside world than she imagined, the narrator does note that this alien world, for all its faults, still has the capacity to instill her with "hope, even longing" (157). That is, even though both worlds are equally real, they are not equally flawed or equally desirable. From the narrator's perspective, the world behind the wall is superior to the outside world because it still holds out the promise of open-ended possibilities, of free choice—of change. The outside world, on the other hand, holds very little promise of a future, let alone a promise of possibilities and free choice. Significantly, when life on the outside becomes intolerable, it is the world behind the wall that nourishes the narrator. Although she tells us that "it was hard to maintain a knowledge of that other world, with its scents and running waters," she does manage to do so (159). As a result, "intimations of that life, or lives, became more powerful and frequent in 'ordinary' life, as if that place were feeding and sustaining us, and wished us to know it" (159). Finally, one day she is able to see a "hidden pattern" on the wall that tells her it is time to gather her charges and take refuge in her alternate world (211).

But even as she enters this world, she is unable to describe it except in general terms as a "place which might present us with anything" (212). The person she "had been looking for all this time was there," but the narrator is unable "to say clearly what she was like" (213). Just as she tries to describe it, this new world seems to fold "itself up around her," seems to be collapsing "into another order of world altogether" (213). In other words, even as we join the narrator and the children as they escape into another dimension, we are not certain what it is we are entering. We are not certain because the narrator herself is not certain. Although she spends considerable time behind the wall and presumably is writing her memoirs from there, it is almost impossible for us to figure out exactly where, or even what, it is.[16] This may frustrate us, but I think Lessing intentionally leaves us without answers. She does not expect us to know where we are because she does not want us to inhabit the world behind the wall in any literal sense. What she is interested in are the visits themselves, those narrative experiences whereby she hopes to unravel our concepts of reality.

In the narrator's accounts of the world outside the flat and the one behind the wall, we are given information that is intended to provide us with new perspectives on our present world and our present view of reality. This is the technique of recognition, where, by sufficiently defamiliarizing reality, Lessing helps us to see it in ways we probably never have before. At the same time that she gives us two alternate views of reality, she asks us to weigh their differences and relative merits. It is in this activity, where we compare the two worlds of the text, that we begin the process of re-cognition, as one of the questions the text inevitably asks is which reality, given the narrator's dilemma, would we choose for ourselves. The process of re-cognition is deepened by the fact that the world behind the wall remains incompletely described and mysterious. So even as we weigh the merits of the two worlds, we are trying to comprehend the meaning of the world behind the wall.[17] If, through the efforts of the narrator, Lessing can get us—if for only a moment—to believe in the existence of an alien world, she will have been successful in getting us to rethink some basic ideas we have about what constitutes reality. If she can get us—again, if for only a moment—to choose the world the narrator chooses, she will have succeeded in leading us to a new view of the world. This is a world where fundamental change remains possible, where reality is not defined by conventional views of time and space. It is a world we cannot enter but only hope to know.

Although we certainly do want to know more about this world, we are rewarded in the novel not by finding answers to our questions but by *trying* to find them, by trying to work through the problem, even though for us there may be no solution. In this case, our reward is different from that of the narrator. Because she is apparently able to work through the intellectual problems posed by the alien world behind the wall, she is eventually able to live there. Because we cannot work through them satisfactorily, our only reward is one of changed perceptions whereby we learn to see our own world quite differently. But at the same time, somehow we are already living behind the wall when the narrator begins her memoirs, a fictional fact she indicates by referring to us as "we." Nor does our salvation as readers end there. Because of the emphasis she places on her own narration, her memoirs imply that her ability to enter strange new dimensions is somehow related to the fact that she is a writer, which suggests that writing has saved her life. By extension, this suggests that somehow reading can save ours, which brings us back full circle to what we have learned from reading this novel.

In summary, just as she did in *Briefing for a Descent into Hell*, Lessing is asking us, her readers, to question, always question, the conventions of our current worldview. At the same time she asks us to question the very form in which she has chosen to write. By using an uncertain narrator, Lessing establishes from the outset that this science fiction novel is as much about the writing and reading of the genre as it is a commentary on social mythology. It is a text that simultaneously asks us to accept and reject its story line. On one level, it asks us to accept what the narrator is saying as real; this makes it conventional science fiction, with the narrator recording what she actually experienced. On another, the text invites us to consider the narrator's story as only a metaphor and to focus our attention on the narration itself. The narrator will be successful, in her own terms, if she gets us to believe that she visits and eventually inhabits the world behind the wall. The author will be successful if she gets us, through the reading process itself, to revise our limited conceptions of what is real, what is possible. As author, Lessing is not asking us literally to walk through walls, therefore, but she is asking us to break through the walls of our conventional thinking—to dismiss our preconceived ideas about reality. In short, she has given us another quintessential Sufi teaching story, in which what is important is not the content of her book but what it does, as real experience, to our heads.

Whether or not Lessing is successful in transforming our perceptions depends largely on whether or not her narrator can loosen our stubborn grip on conventional reality long enough for us to experience an alternative reality. Paradoxically, the narrator gains credibility for her account by openly admitting the reservations she had herself when faced with the fact of an alternate world; she maintains her credibility by further admitting that her perception of events was neither respectable nor official. Rather than relying on official approval, the narrator takes her authority from her own sense of personal responsibility, in the conviction that what an individual does is important to the welfare of others.[18] She contrasts this idea of self-respect to the concept of "it," which she defines as "the word for helpless ignorance, or of helpless awareness" that emerges when people allow faceless bureaucrats to determine their fate for them (151). As long as the people in her neighborhood are able to keep "it" at bay, she reports, "Everything worked. Worked somehow" (180). But once they admit their dependence on an anonymous, absent force, they are doomed. Because she herself has accepted responsibility for Emily, she has earned the right to renounce the beleaguered old world for a bright new one.

Because she has also taken on the responsibility of her readers, we are able to join her in her moment of illumination and grace when she finally takes leave of this world. Her word carries weight with us because, unlike Charles Watkins, she is the only narrative voice in the novel and thus the only authority that we have. In this novel there is no one else speaking for the primacy of known reality. Adding to her credibility is the fact that the Survivor is not penalized for her vision of wholeness but richly rewarded for it. That is, at the end of her story, she does not lose sight of the promised land as Charles does; instead she has earned the right to inhabit it permanently. As Charles's fate suggests Lessing's doubts and pessimism, the Survivor's fate suggests Lessing's growing conviction that her vision is correct and capable of being realized. But by locating this vision in an alternate reality, Lessing continues to suggest that those who accept her vision of wholeness will not find a home in this fragmented, frightened world.

NOTES

1. On page 124, Emily reports a conversation she had with Gerald, during which she asked him, speaking of the narrator, " 'can *she* come' " (emphasis added). This, as far as I can determine, is the only place in the novel where the narrator indicates what her sex is. Doris Lessing, *The Memoirs of a Survivor* (London: Octagon Press, Ltd., 1974; New York: Alfred A. Knopf, 1975); all subsequent page references appear in the text.

Of additional interest regarding the identity of the narrator is Lessing's continued assertion that this novel is "an attempt at autobiography"—first seen on the dust jacket and reiterated during her recent speaking tour of North America; see Roberta Rubenstein, "An Evening at the 92nd Street Y," *Doris Lessing Newsletter*, 8, no. 2 (Fall 1984), 6.

2. This pattern seems to be broken only by the narrator of the fifth book in the series *The Sentimental Agents*; all the others in some fashion or another speak for us, if only to represent our needs to their superiors.

3. Bernard Duyfhuizen examines the implications of the fact that this text is a "consciously written object" in "On the Writing of Future-History: Beginning the Ending in Doris Lessing's *The Memoirs of a Survivor*," (*Modern Fiction Studies*, 26, no. 1 [Spring 1980], 149). For another look at the relationship between reader and text in this novel, see Dagmar Barnouw, "How to Enter an Alien World: Doris Lessing's *Memoirs of a Survivor* and Joanna Russ' *The Two of Them*," presented at the December 1980 MLA as part of the panel "Strategies for Reading Doris Lessing."

4. See, for example, the passage in the first Yellow Notebook where Anna admits to having had trouble writing an accurate account of what had happened years ago at the Mashopi Hotel. Doris Lessing, *The Golden Notebook* (1962; rpt. New York: Bantam, 1973), 228.

5. For a discussion of this phenomenon, see Michael Polanyi, "The Unaccountable Element in Science," in his *Knowing and Being: Essays by*

Michael Polanyi, ed. Marjorie Grene (Chicago: The University of Chicago Press, 1969), 105-20. In this essay he discusses "our tendency to overlook things that are unprecedented. Having no clue to them, we do not see them" (113). On this same subject, see also Kenneth Burke, "Terministic Screens," in his *Language as Symbolic Action: Essays on Life, Literature, and Method* (1966; rpt. Berkeley: University of California Press, 1973), 44-62, in which he notes that "much that we take as observations about 'reality' may be but the spinning out of possibilities implicit in our particular choice of terms" (46).

6. On the inseparability of formal and informal language forms in physics, especially as it pertains to the work and discourse of Einstein and Heisenberg, see David Bohm and D. L. Schumacher, "On the Role of Language Forms in Theoretical and Experimental Physics," in manuscript form, a copy of which is in my possession.

7. On this subject, see, for example, Peter L. Berger and Thomas Luckmann, *The Social Construction of Reality: A Treatise in the Sociology of Knowledge* (1966; rpt. New York: Anchor Books, 1967); Owen Barfield, *Saving the Appearances: A Study in Idolatry* (New York: Harcourt, Brace & World, 1965); and David Bohm, *Wholeness and the Implicate Order* (1980; rpt. London: Routledge & Kegan Paul, 1981).

8. Of Emily's role in this novel, Roberta Rubenstein suggests that she functions for the narrator "as a mediator among different regions of consciousness" (*The Novelistic Vision of Doris Lessing: Breaking the Forms of Consciousness* [Urbana: University of Illinois Press, 1979], 225).

9. Bernard Duyfhuizen reads "the observation point of the narrator's ground-floor flat [as] an interface between the happenings on the 'street' and the 'personal' interior world of the narrator's consciousness, depicted by the world behind the wall" ("On the Writing of Future-History," 151).

10. The world of *Memoirs* also sounds like that described in *The Four-Gated City* just before the holocaust, when, according to Francis Coldridge, *"nothing worked"* (1969; rpt. New York: Bantam Books, 1970), 604; Lessing's emphasis. Of the similarities between the two novels, Roberta Rubenstein writes that "the extrapolation from present realities into an imagined future enables Lessing to frame both a judgment of and a prescription for the alternatives of the future" (*The Novelistic Vision of Doris Lessing*, 220). In her Jungian reading of this novel, Lorelei Cederstrom challenges the science fiction and futuristic interpretations of *Memoirs*, regarding its external images as symbols of the inner landscape (" 'Inner Space' Landscape: Doris Lessing's *Memoirs of a Survivor*," *Mosaic*, 13, nos. 3-4 [Spring-Summer 1980], 115-32). In defense of my own interpretation, I would refer readers to Lessing's statement that she sees "inner space and outer space as reflections of each other. . . . Just as we are investigating subatomic particles and the outer limits of the planetary

system—the large and the small simultaneously—so the inner and the outer are connected" (quoted in Lesley Hazleton, "Doris Lessing on Feminism, Communism and 'Space Fiction,' " *New York Times Magazine*, 25 July 1982, p. 28). The projections of the future that she imagines here are not to be separated from our inner lives; they are in fact a warning of what we will create externally if we do not change our inner selves.

11. In this interpretation I differ from Betsy Draine who argues in "Changing Frames: Doris Lessing's *Memoirs of a Survivor*" that Lessing fails to get her readers to shift between worlds because the second world "is neither vivid to the senses nor compelling to the emotions"; as a result, Draine believes that we end up in "a repudiation of the text as a whole" (*Studies in the Novel*), 11, no. 1 [Spring 1979], 59, 57).

12. For a discussion of this concept see chapter 7, "Convention and Naturalization," in Jonathan Culler's *Structuralist Poetics: Structuralism, Linguistics, and the Study of Literature* (1975; rpt. New York: Cornell University Press, 1982), 131-60. According to Culler, naturalization, as compared to similar terms such as recuperation, motivation, and *vraisemblablisation*, "emphasizes the fact that the strange or deviant is brought within a discursive order and thus made to seem natural" (137).

13. See Nancy Shields Hardin, "The Sufi Teaching Story and Doris Lessing," *Twentieth Century Literature*, 23, no. 3 (October 1977), 323. For a Sufi reading of *Memoirs*, see Ann Scott, "The More Recent Writings: Sufism, Mysticism and Politics," in *Notebooks/ Memoirs/ Archives: Reading and Rereading Doris Lessing*, ed. Jenny Taylor (Boston and London: Routledge & Kegan Paul, 1982), 164-90.

14. In her Jungian reading of *Memoirs*, Roberta Rubenstein argues that the "analogue of rooms becomes the shaping metaphor of the entire novel, taking the metaphoric form of the three-tiered geography developed in *The Four-Gated City*: room, flat (or house), and city, corresponding to intrapsychic, interpersonal, and public dimensions of experience" (*The Novelistic Vision of Doris Lessing*, 221-22).

15. Rubenstein describes the narrator's task as being "not simply to turn her back on a fragmenting outer reality to indulge exclusively in the exploration of her inner landscape, but to reconcile the complementary dimensions of private and social experience, and to find a positive form for them within her own consciousness in order to survive" (*The Novelistic Vision of Doris Lessing*, 224).

16. In *"The Memoirs of a Survivor*: Lessing's Notes Toward a Supreme Fiction," Alvin Sullivan takes the view that "We accept the impossibilities of the novel precisely because the author refuses to discuss them" (*Modern Fiction Studies*, 26, no. 1 [Spring 1980], 159).

17. As Ellen Cronan Rose explains it, "What *The Memoirs of a Survivor* does is to challenge the *reader* to accomplish this task [of integrating two

worlds]. Its ending demands that we abandon our accustomed notions of what is real, enlarging our definition of reality by incorporating the contents of experience we cannot rationally understand" ("The End of the Game: New Directions in Doris Lessing's Fiction," *Journal of Narrative Technique*, 6, no. 1 [Winter 1976], 74). Similarly, Alvin Sullivan notes that the "ending Lessing offers is the ultimate ending, the supreme fiction that all discover," wherein we are restored "to knowledge of ourselves" ("Lessing's Notes," 160).

18. In this respect, the narrator exemplifies the kind of artist that Lessing describes in "The Small Personal Voice"—the person who accepts responsibility for the welfare of others. See the discussions in the introduction and chapter 1 above and the essay itself in *Declaration*, ed. by Tom Maschler (c. 1957; New York: E. P. Dutton & Co., 1958), 187-201.

3.

Out of Opposition:
Re: Colonised Planet 5, Shikasta

If Lessing introduces us to a new world in *The Memoirs of a Survivor*, she reintroduces us to the old one in her *Canopus in Argos: Archives* series (1979-). She does so by inventing an alien, yet disturbingly familiar, cosmology, through which she retells much of human history. In this series, which to date contains five volumes, Lessing has imagined the existence of several different planets—all of which defamiliarize life on earth.[1] Throughout history these planets have been the scene of conflict among three galactic empires: Canopus in Argos, which stands for harmony and benevolence and gives the series its name; Shammat, which represents evil and corruption and is a planet in the empire of Puttiora; and Sirius, which is a technologically advanced empire of ambitious bureaucrats who periodically invade other planets to enlarge their territory. In order to influence the history of civilization, these empires regularly send envoys planetside. According to this cosmology, our world has never been free of these competing missionaries who through the millennia have deeply affected the course of human civilization, including our sacred, profane, and natural histories. Because of this premise, most of the recognition that takes place as we read these five novels is that of a religious, political, or scientific nature—as in Lessing's retelling we recognize material familiar to us from other, more conventional sources. Although it is familiar, it is also strange, presented as it is from a wholly alien point of view.

Because of its alien perspectives, *Canopus in Argos* takes us on a rhetorical journey that challenges most of the fundamental beliefs we hold about the universe and our place in it. In fact, if we were to take her metaphors at face value, our view of the universe would be as shaken as was the Ptolemaic view by the Copernican revolution 400 years ago.[2] Lessing's new cosmology, of course, unlike that of Copernicus, is without any empirical basis; it has its existence only in the imagination—as Lessing reminds us in the preface to *The Sirian Experiments*. In what is apparently a response to queries on the subject, Lessing here assures her readers that no, she does "not 'believe' that there is a planet called Shammat full of low-grade space pirates . . . nor that we are the scene of conflicts between those great empires Canopus and Sirius."[3] But even if she does not literally believe in Canopus or expect us to, her fiction can have a liberating effect on our imagination just as the discoveries of Copernicus had on the closed thinking of the sixteenth century. That is, it too can help usher in a renaissance of attitudes and thinking about our place in the universe. It can also serve to remind us that we are indeed a minor planet around a minor sun—a small part of an unimaginably large system, the origins and purpose of which, even in an age of unprecedented scientific discovery, continue to elude us. But even if, cosmically speaking, we are small and insignificant, we are still, as this series makes clear, worth saving and capable of the evolutionary changes needed for survival.

Because Lessing has taken a cosmic stance in these novels, there are very few fully realized characters for us to identify with in it. This development, which was certainly foreshadowed in *Briefing for a Descent into Hell*, has been a disappointment to many of her readers who have valued her work as much for her characterization as her ideas.[4] I have spoken with some, in fact, who have confessed ruefully that they can no longer read her work, that they have been able to find nothing in *Canopus in Argos* to engage their fancy. As I suggested earlier, what these readers will find in *Canopus in Argos*, if not the emotional involvement they have come to expect, is a dialectical exchange or cognitive engagement through which they can participate with Lessing in the destruction of old worlds and the creation of new ones. Lessing's own enthusiasm for the genre is clear from her prefatory remarks to *Shikasta* (1979), the first novel of the new series. Here, perhaps anticipating that she might be criticized for writing science fiction, she tells us that she originally began the novel thinking that when it was complete she "would be done with the subject."[5] But, instead as she wrote she "was invaded with ideas for other books, other stories, and the exhilaration that comes from being set free into a larger scope, with more capacious possibilities and themes" (ix). In this "new world" that she invented for herself, she found she had been "set free to be as experimental . . . and as traditional" as she liked (ix). This statement suggests that those who read *Canopus in Argos* as *science* but not *serious* fiction are missing the point, as obviously she has intended it to be both. Lessing herself indirectly confirms her own cross-generic intentions in her spirited defense of Olaf Stapledon when she asserts that "there is something very wrong with an attitude that puts a 'serious' novel on one shelf and, let's say *First and Last Men* [*sic*] on another" (x). By implication, these remarks also admonish us not to categorize her work, for such labeling would only serve to limit our understanding of her series.

Lessing also uses her preface to notify us ahead of time that even if *Canopus in Argos* is not strictly conventional, it is still recognizably traditional. For example, she specifically identifies the Old Testament as the "starting point" of *Shikasta* (x). And in subsequent novels she openly borrows from the Sufi and Taoist traditions, structuring the entire work as a collection of spiritual teaching stories. But the major literary tradition behind Lessing's series is, of course, that of science and/or space fiction. Beyond her remarks about Olaf Stapledon, there are echoes of other possible influences from such diverse works as George Orwell's *1984* (1949), Arthur C. Clarke's *Childhood's End* (1953), Frank Herbert's *Dune* series (begun in 1965), John Brunner's *The Sheep Look Up* (1972), Dorothy Bryant's *The Kin of Ata Are Waiting for You* (1976), Marge Piercy's *Woman on the Edge of Time* (1976), and Ian Watson's *Miracle Visitors* (1978). When Lessing speaks of being as experimental and as traditional as she liked in this series, therefore, it would appear that she is referring to the fact that she has drawn on many different literary traditions in order to forge her own synergistic vision of cosmic wholeness.

That Lessing is also alluding to formal experimentation, of course, is evident immediately in the structure of *Shikasta*. But it is also evident in the kind of series she is writing, as it is non-linear, taking its coherence not from a single story line but from the ideas it expresses. As such it invites several questions about the relationship of the individual texts to one another and to the series itself. Yet another possible conjunction of the experimental and the traditional that Lessing might have in mind here has to do with the fact that this series, like so much of her writing, has been strongly influenced by the Marxist literary tradition—a tradition to which Lessing has giving new life and meaning by dispensing with much of its political dogma and retaining its intellectual and critical methodology. For unlike so many early *Marxist* writers who dispensed with methodology and retained dogma, Lessing demonstrates that the strength in *Marxian* thinking lies in its dialectical process. Lessing's most successful experimentation in this series, therefore, might very well be her application of traditional Marxian methodology to both apocalyptic and utopian science fiction.[6]

The influence of Marxian dialectics is certainly not to be overlooked in *Shikasta*. Its influence is so pervasive one could assert, with very little exaggeration, that virtually everything in this novel participates in a dialectic of one kind or another, whether it be the dialectics of form or content. Because Lessing has so fully realized here the dialectical possibilities inherent in science fiction, she has made of this novel one of her most effective vehicles of social criticism to date. Here, as she did in her earlier fiction, she lays bare the myths of manifest destiny and Western superiority that have corrupted our souls and threaten the very existence of life itself. But not only does *Shikasta* depict the dangers of twentieth-century life, its dialectics offer a way out of the situation through the process of cognitive engagement—the narrative imperative that virtually forces us out of our comfortable, conventional fictions which we continue to mistake for reality. Like the rest of Lessing's science fiction, this novel challenges us not just emotionally but also intellectually and epistemologically. It asks nothing less than for us to join it in redefining reality itself. In this respect, it seems to go beyond the demands of Lessing's more conventional fiction, which (strange as it may seem) does ask less of us.

Much like Stapledon's *Last and First Men*, *Shikasta* is narrated by an alien visitor to earth—a literary device that Lessing used in her 1971 story "Report on the Threatened City."[7] Like his counterpart, the narrator of *Shikasta* has also been sent to earth to report on its condition and help its people. But Johor's mission extends far beyond that of warning a single city of imminent danger. He and the other emissaries from the star system Canopus in Argos have been given the task of maintaining the already weakened bond between earth and its benevolent overlords. As the narrative opens, Shikasta, which is the name given earth by these aliens, is being devitalized by the malevolent forces of Shammat and by a falling away from the Canopean values of spiritual and social unity. Because this is a time of particular danger to the planet—a time late in the twentieth century—Johor, one of the more experienced of the Empire's envoys, has been assigned to return to Shikasta to try to counter the forces of evil. Before setting out, he prepares a document in which he tries to explain to Canopean skeptics just why this self-destructive world "*is* worth so much of our time and trouble" (3; Lessing's emphasis). This document constitutes roughly half of the novel. It is supplemented by material provided by the Canopean Archivists who have "edited" it for the instruction of "first-year students of Canopean Colonial Rule." Although, as the presence of these editors suggests, Johor is not the only narrator of *Shikasta*, he is its informing consciousness. This is confirmed in the text and in the full title of the book: *Re: Colonised Planet 5, Shikasta: Personal, Psychological, Historical Documents Relating to Visit by JOHOR (George Sherban), Emissary (Grade 9) 87th of the Period of the Last Days.*

Shikasta is divided into two parts. The first part runs from page 3 to page 210 and ends with the birth of Johor into the body of a human being named George Sherban. The second part runs from page 210 to page 365 and ends with a report on George's activities after the end of World War III. Both sections are replete with supplemental material, such as the Archivists' notes, reports from other agents, and selections from the official *History of Shikasta.* The first part is narrated by Johor just before his incarnation as George Sherban and consists mainly of reports he made during previous visits to Shikasta and of painful memories he has heretofore been able to suppress. The second section, titled "Documents Relating to George Sherban (Johor)," is separated from the first by two bold horizontal lines and consists of secondhand accounts of his activities during his visit in "The Period of the Last Days." These accounts primarily take the form of a diary kept by

George's sister, Rachel Sherban, and a series of letters and reports written by an overlord of the Chinese government, an ambitious administrator named Chen Liu. These two sections, as I shall discuss later, constitute a major dialectic structure within the novel, whereby Lessing generates a debate in her readers' minds as to which views of reality will be accepted as normative—those expressed by Johor or those expressed by Rachel and Chen Liu.

Not only is the novel as a whole structured dialectically, but part one features its own internal dialectics. These dialectics stem from the fact that Johor is simultaneously addressing two audiences. Like the narrators who follow him in the series, Johor is at once an unself-conscious narrator and a self-conscious one. As he pleads with his fellow Canopeans that the planet is worth saving, he quite unconsciously addresses us. As he does so, he unwittingly but effectively functions as our guide-leader, mediating between our conventional view of reality and Lessing's alternative view. Because of the fact that what one audience takes for granted the other has never heard of, Johor's task could be a monumental one, resulting in all sorts of narrative dilemmas. But Lessing has turned the dilemma to advantage by using it as an occasion for recognition. In order for Johor to explain what he perceives to be our totally irrational behavior, he must make clear to his eminently reasonable Canopean audience what life on this poor damaged planet is like. In making it clear to them, Johor, because of his alien perspective, necessarily defamiliarizes it for us. This is where the bulk of the novel's recognition comes in, therefore, as we are handed information in part one that has been taken out of context, given an alien interpretation (not to mention alien names), and occasionally twisted to the point where it refutes what we know of objective reality.

Before we examine this defamiliarization in depth, however, we need first to consider the consequences of the dialectical exchanges between us and Johor's narration. Because we are practically forced to notice how the novel has been constructed, inevitably we become self-conscious readers and the novel becomes a rhetorical text.[8] Lessing reinforces our self-consciousness by making Johor a self-conscious narrator—one who, like the narrator of *The Memoirs of a Survivor* before him, finds it difficult to explain things to his story audience. Where the Survivor struggles to explain an alien world to human beings, Johor struggles to explain human beings to an alien world. His difficulties are compounded by the fact that the life expectancies and mental capacities of his peers far exceed those of his subjects. At one point, midway through his report, when he is trying to explain how forgetful of Canopean laws human beings have become, he exclaims fretfully, "How can I describe it? Only with difficulty, to Canopeans!" (72). Cognizant of the vast difference between his audience and his subject, he supplements his report with additional information. But this material also reflects the same problem of superior minds trying in vain to understand inferior ones. The summary chapter of *History of Shikasta*, for example, reminds Canopeans that "it is nearly impossible for people with whole minds . . . to understand the mentation of Shikastans" (85). Because we are the Shikastans in question here and because we are the narrative's one and only *real* audience, these passages where Johor and the historians are in effect complaining about how hard it is to describe us to ourselves cannot help but make us self-conscious readers—thus increasing both our estrangement from the text and our re-cognition as we try to combat this estrangement by somehow reconciling Johor's perspective with our own. Whether we accept his as it is or try to adjust ours to fit it, the result is the same: we have begun to rethink reality.

Another technique that Lessing uses to call attention to her novel as novel is what I call inter-textual recognition. That is, there are several places in *Shikasta*—and in subsequent novels—that recall and re-construct passages from Lessing's earlier fiction. For example, in the passage cited above where Johor complains about the mentation of Shikastans, he also remarks on their amazing capacity for self-delusion. This self-delusion has to do with the Shikastans' ability to believe, even in the face of imminent global disaster, "that 'on the whole' all was well" (86). For those who remember Lessing's "Report on the Threatened City," this passage will have the ring of familiarity, as in this story her astral messengers are dumbfounded to learn that people would continue to live without fear in a city they know for certain is in danger of being destroyed at any time by a massive earthquake. Another example of inter-textual recognition takes place when we read Johor's definition of nostalgia and realize it could have come straight out of *The Golden Notebook*. Johor describes it as a "longing for what has never been, or at least not in the form and shape imagined" (5-6). Anna Wulf describes it as "a longing for licence, for freedom, for the jungle, for formlessness."[9]

If these were the only examples of inter-textual recognition, they would not be very remarkable, of course, as the work of most authors shows similar congruence. But the recognition does not end here. There is, for example, additional correspondence between *Shikasta* and *Briefing for a Descent into Hell*, extensive enough to leave the impression that we are supposed to think of them together. It will be recalled, for example, that on their voyage in the Atlantic, Charles and his companions set out to look for a mysterious "*Them*"—for in "waiting for *Them* lies all your hope."[10] The Crystal "They" travel in, which represents perfect unity, contains "*crystallisations of the substance* which were its functions, its reason for being, its creatures" (78). In *Shikasta*, Johor uses similar images to describe what it is like for his friend Ben to wait for rescue in Zone Six. This zone, one of many that surround Shikasta, seems to function as something of a way station for those souls who have not yet completed their tasks on Shikasta and must, therefore, suffer through multiple reincarnations. Like Charles, who himself falls away from his true purpose in coming to earth, those who are in Zone Six have in their lifetime "succumbed to Shikasta, [have] suffered some failure of purpose or will, and [have] been expelled back to this place" (9). While Ben is there, hoping to free himself of the anguish of rebirth on Shikasta, he vows to "*crystallise into a substance* that could survive and withstand" the temptations of "self-indulgence and weakness" (9). Because avoiding these temptations is almost impossible, Ben and the others have given up, have become "thin miserable ghosts, yearning and hungering for '*Them*' who would come for them, would lift them out and away from this terrible place" (9; my emphases throughout).

Another example of the correspondence between the two novels occurs in their prophetic account of how the technological excesses of the late twentieth century have insured the destruction of the world. A sampling of the lengthy descriptions from *Briefing* includes the following phrases that have counterparts in *Shikasta*. According to what Charles reports, "men had poisoned all the oceans and rivers so that beasts and fish were dying there" (90); as a result of the war between the apes and rat-dogs, the two groups become "crazy," their eyes become "reddened, and their fur and hide roughened and dirty" (95); everywhere he looks Charles sees "fishes and sea-creatures floating bellies up, and on the sea were patches of oil, dark mineral-smelling" (96). According to the *History of Shikasta*, at this time the "earth was being despoiled, . . . the seas filled with filth and poison, the atmosphere was corrupted. . . . These were maddened creatures" (90).[11]

As close as these correspondences are between *Shikasta* and *Briefing*, there is a still closer one between *Shikasta* and *The Four-Gated City* in the person of Lynda Coldridge. Although she is but a minor character in *Shikasta*, appearing as she does for only about ten pages, her appearance in and of itself is noteworthy as it provides a striking example of inter-textual recognition. Here, there is no doubt that we are being asked to recall another text. One effect of this recognition, as well as the others described previously, is to help unify Lessing's work by reminding us of the congruence and development of her ideas from novel to novel. In a way the recognition also functions as a kind of literary allusion, deepening the meaning of an individual passage by referring us to another, similar one found in another novel. At the same time, the parallel passages also function rhetorically to make us even more aware of the novel as a fabrication. For recognizing familiar passages or even, as in this case, familiar characters, is both rewarding and unsettling to the reader. It is rewarding because when we see something we recognize, we are pleased by our ability to see parallels from work to work. In the alien environs of a novel like *Shikasta*, furthermore, it is also rewarding—not to mention epistemologically reassuring—to find something that helps us get our bearings.

And yet, even as we take comfort in the familiar, it is downright unsettling to encounter a character from another novel—a novel that is not part of the series we are reading. It is somehow a violation of the conventions of non-serial fiction for us to be presented with an extra-textual character. On the one hand, by introducing a character from another novel, the author asks us to accept her as real—real enough to move about from work to work.

But, on the other hand, because we know her only as a character in another novel, the device becomes ultimately an artificial one, forcing us once again to become conscious of the rhetorical qualities of the text we are reading. (This is similar to reading a novel in which a character is reading a novel that we recognize; we cannot come upon this detail without temporarily stepping out of the world of the text.) When we find an entire section in *Shikasta* that has been written by Lynda Coldridge, therefore, we are pleasantly surprised to see her (a pleasure that is deepened by the fact that there are so few characters at all in the novel and so any we discover are welcome), and at the same time we are disconcerted by her appearance. But because this is a novel that derives much of its effectiveness from getting us to recognize things that make us uncomfortable, the fact of our being disconcerted is surely the point.

Not insignificantly, the passages on Lynda Coldridge deal with her so-called mental illness and the fact that she willingly agreed "to risk her sanity . . . for the benefit of others" (178). Because of the negative attitudes of society toward the mentally ill, however, Lynda's decision has brought her much anguish—an anguish the novel implies was entirely unnecessary. Rejecting the pathological explanation of mental illness, the novel suggests that the so-called insane among us have simply lost the ability to screen out the excess information that daily bombards us all. Rather than hearing voices that are not there, the "insane" hear voices that *are* there. Because the rest of us "are machines set to accept only . . . 5 percent" of this information, we have erroneously concluded that this 5 percent constitutes the "whole universe" (183). Lynda is convinced that she herself "was born a 6 percent person, not mad at all" (186). But because she was willing to admit to her visions, she has been treated by society as though she were indeed insane. In reviewing Lynda's case one more time, Lessing is able once again to chide society for its paranoid reaction to the mentally ill. But, more important, she is also able to remind us about the relationship between madness and the evolution of sensory capacities—a relationship she graphically described in the earlier novel. She reminds us of their relationship because it is relevant to the kinds of mental exercises she would have us undergo in *Shikasta*. Through this inter-textual recognition, she also reminds us of the personal sacrifices, and possible dangers, involved in exploring new territory, especially the uncharted territories of the human mind.

By repeating the same criticism of society from novel to novel, Lessing suggests just how difficult it is for us to make any progress or for us to learn from the past—something that itself provides another occasion for inter-textual recognition. In *Shikasta*, Johor asks quite rhetorically of human beings, "What is the point of learning so much, so painfully . . . if the next generation . . . can accept nothing as 'given,' as learned, as already understood?" (174). In "The Temptation of Jack Orkney," the title character draws the same rueful conclusion about how impossible it is for one generation to help the next. During a mid-life crisis, this aging liberal-activist despairs because he suddenly sees that his son "would have to make the identical journey he and his contemporaries had made, to learn lessons exactly as if they had never been learned before."[12] It is against this pattern of failure that Lessing struggles in order to teach us the lessons of history. If she is to succeed where others have failed in this thankless mission, she must not only give us the information we need but she must also teach us how to use it. She must teach us how to avoid the traps of the old ways of thinking. One way she shocks us out of indifference is by making us self-conscious readers—by making us continually aware of the fact that we are indeed reading a novel and a didactic one at that. She also makes us self-conscious readers by holding before us a textual mirror that is intended both to distort and reflect what we know of reality. It is a mirror that alienates us in its distortions and frightens us in its accuracy.

Some of the first realities that are challenged in *Shikasta* are grounded in the natural and physical sciences, as though Lessing were impressing upon us the relativity of even our empirically established truths. Thus the very premise of the series violates Darwin's theory of evolution. Instead of Darwin's scientifically based theories, we are asked here to accept the alternative explanation that, ever since this planet could support higher life forms, it has been under the control and guardianship of envoys from the Canopean and Sirian Empires, who between them have been responsible for changing the direction of human evolution through programs of instruction and selective breeding. In addition to violating what we know of natural history, the series also violates what we know of the physical sciences, as six inhabitable, apparently contiguous zones are described as surrounding the planet. Furthermore, we are asked to believe that "Canopus" is not just the second brightest star in the night sky, located in the constellation Argo Navis, but also the name of a race of super beings who have taken on themselves the benevolent supervision of several planets. Whether in fact there are Canopeans (who would not call themselves this anyway) living on planets circling Canopus, we have no way of knowing. That earth might have been visited by these extra-terrestrial envoys we also cannot confirm—the efforts of Erich von Däniken notwithstanding. Besides having no scientific validity, the fact that these supposed super beings have supervised the course of human history also violates our Western religious myths that attribute any so-called extra-terrestrial visitation to that of God's angels. Lessing compounds our disbelief by identifying other envoys as being from the Sirian Empire, when we know Sirius to be the brightest star in the constellation Canis Major. In short, what Lessing's narrators present to their story audiences as fact is nothing more than fancy to us. But it is fancy that has a purpose beyond beguiling us. By using a traditional science fiction convention—that of having imaginary aliens visit earth from real stars—Lessing is able simultaneously to defamiliarize our physical reality, cast doubt on our science, revise our theory of evolution, rewrite our religious myths, and call attention to the rhetorical quality of her texts.

As we have already seen, Lessing states in her prefatory remarks to *Shikasta* that this novel "has as its starting point, like many others of the genre, the Old Testament" (x). And indeed, without too much difficulty, we recognize in it many defamiliarized allusions to this ancient work. On one of Johor's earlier visits, for example, he encounters someone Lessing quite disingenuously has named David, who himself not uncoincidentally is a "storyteller and song-maker" (49). Johor meets David after the departure of the Giants, a superior race of beings whom Canopus had imported from Colony 10 to tutor the indigenous inhabitants of Shikasta. If David is a clear reference to the Old Testament, the giants are a less obvious one. Although they are given a major role in the early history of Shikasta, in the book of Genesis we learn merely that when

Noah lived there "were giants in the earth in those days" (Genesis 6:4). (This example from *Shikasta* is yet another example of intertextual recognition, as Charles Watkins has also quoted this Biblical passage; see *Briefing*, p. 11.) In the same verse of Genesis, there is also an account of the "sons of God" mating with the "daughters of men," another passage that seems to assume more importance in *Shikasta* than it does in the Bible, as it is described in some detail by another Canopean envoy (98). This envoy also refers to the Covenant God made with Noah, but in this version the pact originates with Canopean envoys who use the natural disaster to teach humanity that it must not be tempted again into a "falling away into wickedness and evil practice" (100). Other incidental details from the Old Testament that appear in the novel refer to the Tower of Babel (101) and the birth of Ishmael and Isaac (107).

Of more importance to the text is the advent of the true prophets, who in the Old Testament were distinguishable from the false prophets by their unrelenting messages of doom. They proved their identity as prophets, in other words, by telling the people not what they wanted to hear but that they must obey the will of God and turn from sin. According to Lessing's retelling, these prophets, whom she has fittingly renamed the Public Cautioners, were not messengers from God at all but envoys from Canopus—many of whom quite unintentionally left in their wake full-fledged religious institutions (108). In the excerpt from *History of Shikasta* describing the "Period of the Public Cautioners," we learn that the visits of these "Grade I" emissaries had both good and bad issue. On the one hand, they stabilized the cultures they visited; on the other, almost immediately upon the departure of the Canopeans, a manipulative priesthood rose to power with the cooperation of the military (111). If Lessing finds much to criticize in all organized religions, she is at her most unforgiving when it comes to Christianity, as it continually surfaces as Johor's worst-case example. In *Shikasta* he describes Christianity (without ever naming it per se) as being "the most inflexible, the least capable of self-examination," and its marauding disciples unwitting victims themselves of "a religion as bigoted as Shikasta has ever seen" (159).

In focusing on Christianity, Lessing apparently wants to demonstrate how the hierarchy of the church has debased sacred myths and rituals for its own political purposes. Perhaps the best example she offers is in Johor's account of the "Festival of the Child," which is clearly a defamilarized reference to the Holy Child of Prague. According to Johor, the festival originated when an itinerant teacher (probably a Canopean envoy) visited the inhabitants of an isolated village in order to introduce them to "more advanced ideas" of human potential and social equality (164). To reinforce these ideas, the visitor used the example of several different children to proclaim that each one was "a miracle, a wonder . . . [who held] within her, or within him, all the past and all the future" (167-68). After their teacher left, the people initiated a secret ritual to preserve what they could of the stories they had heard. But the local monks regarded this ritual as a threat to their hegemony and tried to ban it. Failing this, they converted it into the Christian ceremony that celebrates only the Christ child and not all children—a ceremony that the priests control. With this example Lessing summarizes her view that, instead of serving the spiritual needs of its people, the church serves primarily the fiscal and political needs of its own bureaucracy.

In these passages where she defamiliarizes our religious myths and rituals, Lessing undertakes several tasks. By indicating that the Canopean agents have been consistently received on earth as prophets or gods, for example, she acknowledges the seemingly universal human need to worship a higher being. Similarly, by showing how humans can invest non-sacred events with religious significance she acknowledges the human hunger for transcendence. But she also reminds us how this hunger plays into the hands of unscrupulous leaders. In other words, she takes the example of a need that in itself is not by definition corrupt or corrupting and shows how, in the context of human ambition and greed, it all too often has led to the perversion of what is most noble in humanity. On another level, by de-mythologizing our religious beliefs, Lessing also invites us to reconsider what we really mean when we claim to abide by religious principles. In getting us to recognize our sacred history in her revised profane version, she tries to help us rethink this aspect of our lives—hoping to force us to join her at the point of re-cognition whereby we too will question the source and structure of many of our moral codes.

If she is concerned in *Shikasta* with the tendency of human beings to pervert what is essentially an ennobling desire, that of believing in a higher being and a higher good, she is also concerned with our tendency to splinter the world into competing factions. In the preface to *Shikasta*, for example, she reminds us that the "sacred literatures of all races and nations have many things in common," leading some scholars to conclude that "there has never been more than one Book in the Middle East" (x, xi). Be this as it may, most of us seem to be intent on finding differences among ourselves—or, where none exist, inventing them. This urge to see ourselves as somehow different from everybody else—and therefore special or superior—characterizes our politics as much as our religions. This similarity and others lead Lessing to conclude that politics is really nothing more than an analogue of religion. Johor reports to his peers, for example, that religion in the twentieth century has become less tyrannical because it has lost most of its "certainties" (196). But the gap that has been left by the weakening of religion has been filled by nationalism, "that pernicious new creed which uses much of the energies that once fed religions" (196). Another creed he identifies is science, describing it as "the most recent of the religions" and, contrary to its initial promise of intellectual freedom, as "bigoted and inflexible as any" of them (197).[13] In short, Lessing has set up a comparison in which politics = religion = science. By placing these three institutions in a complex metaphor, where each one is comparable to the other, Lessing forces us to regard all three from a new perspective, as we are generally unaccustomed to seeing any of the three as synonymous with the others. Through this metaphor she also constructs an image of our world in which these three divisions of reality have been reunited.

Another social myth Lessing works to discredit is that of nationalistic differences. In doing so, she confronts some of our most cherished beliefs. Of the parties that rose to power after World War II, for example, Johor reports that "what was remarkable about this particular time was how much they all resembled each other, while they spent most of their energies in describing and denigrating differences that they imagined existed between them" (78). Of the period between World War I and II, the *History of Shikasta* reports that the two major dictatorships in power at that time (Germany and Russia) "saw each other as enemies, as totally different, as wicked and contemptible—while they behaved in exactly the same way" (85). With these passages

Lessing, speaking from the dispassionate perspective of the immortal beings she has created, calls into question whether or not World War II was worth fighting. She raises the question by dismissing as irrelevant any political differences between Nazi Germany and Soviet Russia—differences that retrospectively are perhaps irrelevant but that at the time were certainly meaningful, especially to the Allies. Her own disenchantment with communism aside, it is clear that these startling passages are intended to challenge our view of recent history. They are part of the opposite term in the dialectic she is setting up between us and her text, a dialectic she hopes to use to forge a new view of reality—including, of course, a new view of world history.

Support for this reading can be found in the passages themselves and in the overall dialectical structure of the novel. In the passages just cited, which are taken from the *History of Shikasta*, the narrative moves from despair to hope in a series of descriptions that defamiliarizes the period between World War I and II, the period the novel identifies as taking place during "The Century of Destruction" (83-93). The section opens with descriptions so totally defamiliarized that we must attend carefully to the text to understand what Lessing is referring to. In order to solve the riddle of the text, we have to begin to see the world as she is describing it; we have to begin to see the two superpowers as virtually identical.[14] The text also challenges our perspective by describing ideologies "which were the same in performance, but so different in self-description" (86). Like the passage cited earlier, this one also virtually identifies science as a political institution, calling it "the most recent ideology" which World War II had "immeasurably strengthened" (88). Comparing the age of technology to a religious reign of terror, this section notes that after the war the "armament industries" became the "real rulers of every geographical area" (86). But because "lies and propaganda *were* government," the people were largely unaware of their subjection (86; Lessing's emphasis). "Never," according to this section, "has there been such a totalitarian, all-pervasive, all-powerful governing caste anywhere: and yet the citizens of Shikasta were hardly aware of it, as they mouthed slogans and waited for their deaths by holocaust" (88).

Although the holocaust comes, Lessing does not portray it as being wholly bad. After establishing a defamiliarized version of the period before and after World War II, she describes in this section the outbreak of World War III. This war is preceded by a widespread discontent among the world's population brought on by the fact that, although consumption was encouraged at an unprecedented level, the people's "real selves, their hidden selves, which were unfed, were ignored, were starved, were lied to, by almost every agency around them, by every authority they had been taught to, but could not, respect" (91). The war itself begins by accident—a mechanical failure. Although 99 percent of the world's population is destroyed by the radiation, poisons, and other agents of death released by the war, the remaining 1 percent are "restored to themselves" and are few enough in number to have sufficient substance-of-we-feeling to "keep them all sweet, and whole, and healthy" (93).

In its contents and in the development of its ideas from despair to hope, this section parallels the novel itself and the section just referred to in which Johor equates religion, politics, and science. Besides setting up his three-term metaphor, Johor's purpose in his "Additional Explanatory Information II" is to describe the need that human beings have had for opiates "to dull the pain of their condition" (195). If these opiates have in the past been moderately effective in keeping fear and reality at bay, they are no longer. Because "the nursery of life itself" is "poisoned," there is also no comfort or salvation even in nature (198). In these passages, which are beautifully elegiac, Johor describes the lot of people who turn to nature for solace only to find that they "cannot rest in thoughts of the great creator, nature" (199). "Nothing they can touch, or see, or handle sustains them, nowhere can they take refuge in the simple good sense of nature" (200). And yet, even in the refuse heap of civilization, there is hope available to those who can see in a single fallen leaf "nature as a roaring creative fire in whose crucible species are born and die and are reborn in every breath" (201-2). Their hope comes from their ability, forged itself in suffering and despair, to see that "the laws that made this shape must be . . . stronger in the end than the slow distorters and perverters of the substance of life" (202). Ultimately, they are "weaned from everything but the knowledge that the universe is a roaring engine of creativity, and they are only temporary manifestations of it" (203). Johor concludes this account of the Shikastan frame of mind with the observation that Shikastans themselves even "in their awful and ignoble end" are able to find in this perspective occasion for hope and patience: "I am putting the word *faith* here," he writes. "After thought. With caution. With an exact and hopeful respect" (203; Lessing's emphasis).

It is in this final part of the section, "Additional Explanatory Information II," I would suggest, that Johor speaks most directly for Lessing and not in the earlier part when he seems to be advocating pacifism at any cost. Although it would be impossible to try to demonstrate that at any point in her fiction Lessing has advocated the necessity of war as public policy, there is also no conclusive evidence to suggest that she herself thinks World War II was fought at the time over negligible differences.[15] When she uses Johor to criticize the pattern of global conflict, therefore, rather than using him to argue against the necessity of having to fight particular wars in the past, Lessing is using him to posit a polar opposite to the kind of behavior and thinking that historically has led to these wars. In taking this position, she is establishing a dialogue between her text and her readers, through which she hopes to make us more conscious of the consequences of our perceptual paradigms, especially those that relate to individualism and nationalism. She is using Johor, in other words, primarily as a mediator between the alien ideas of the text (in this case, that nationalism is an outmoded, conquerable evil that necessarily leads to conflict) and the commonly held ideas of her readers (that nationalism is a self-protective form of social mythology which arises naturally out of the need for people to have a common identity and acts as a kind of shield against outside threats).

The emphasis in the conclusion to Johor's "Additional Explanatory Information II," as in the rest of Lessing's science fiction, is on process, the process in this instance through which human beings, faced with the prospects of utter global destruction, can find faith enough to keep going.[16] In his account, Johor takes us through the process whereby humanity has turned to various religious, political, and scientific institutions for the answer to the question of what it means to be human. But each institution, in turn, has been found wanting. In an era when religion is unable to counter the spiritual crises raised by scientific discoveries and when politics threaten to use these discoveries to destroy the world itself, human beings have been left with virtually no external comforts. When they look to nature, at first they see only a world of vast, empty space—the world that modern physics has introduced us to on a subatomic level. But the passage continues with the remarkable observation that these people "repose in their imaginations on chaos, making strength from the possibilities of a creative destruction" (203). It is here that Lessing draws on the findings of physics to express her own philosophy that the world of everyday reality is a chimera, behind which lies an ultimate reality where everything partakes of everything else. Because human beings are only "temporary manifestations" of the universe, it is possible to take comfort in the fact that life itself, in some form or another, will go on without us—a consolation that anticipates the conclusion to the fourth novel in the series, *The Making of the Representative for Planet 8* (203). Given this almost mystical consolation, it is not inappropriate that Johor concludes this section by referring to *faith.*

As a prophetic writer, Lessing is in the somewhat untenable position of wanting to express hope for the future even as she predicts disaster. Although many of her novels threaten us with the prospects of imminent disaster, the very fact that she is taking the time to warn us about the consequences of our actions suggests that she holds out some hope for us to redeem ourselves in time to turn back the direction of history. In this novel, having predicted yet another holocaust, she tries to find some good in it.[17] It is a daring move, perhaps, as it verges almost on accepting that which she has fought so hard to prevent, but given the social and scientific developments that have accompanied her writing career, perhaps it is not unexpected. Although she and others have bravely voiced their fears, their work has had seemingly little impact on world politics. It is certainly possible that after a lifetime devoted to warning a world determined to ignore even the most eloquent prophets of doom, Lessing would resign herself to the apocalypse and offer her readers consolation for the devastation she sees as inevitable (see chapter 6 below).

But even as she offers us consolation in the form of the imperishable universe, she cannot forego her original impulse to reform us so this consolation might become unnecessary. And, as we might expect of Lessing, the consolations and reforms are of a piece—both centered on the oneness of life. Even though modern physics teaches us that the world is indeed interrelated, most of us are reluctant to accept this fact. In order to counter our skepticism, Lessing uses the device of alien beings to teach us some elemental truths about our home planet. She does this, as we have seen, primarily by defamiliarizing reality for us—practically forcing us to see our world from Johor's alien perspective. At the same time that he defamiliarizes reality for us, Johor is himself an example of defamiliarized reality, as he belongs to both worlds of the text—to this world and to his home planet. In his very being, therefore, he manifests the oneness of life by embodying both familiar and alien qualities.

For his role as representative of both Canopus and Shikasta, Johor is admirably suited, as he is personally familiar with both worlds. He is a citizen of Canopus and has lived as a native on Shikasta, mixing with the people and teaching them Canopean laws. As a Canopean, Johor is several thousand years old, which means that he has been able to visit earth over a period of millennia and his historical reports are therefore firsthand. He is, indeed, the ideal witness and guide-leader because he was present at many of the key events in the history of the world. But during these times, even in his human form, he has not been limited to a single point of view. In his combination of Canopean and Shikastan qualities, he has eluded the danger of focusing too narrowly on events, a danger that is described in the text as part of "Notes on Planet Shikasta for Guidance of Colonial Servants." These notes remind prospective emissaries, "On the scale of the electron Shikasta appears as empty space" (6). (This implies, of course, that our view of history, compared to the Canopean one, is like that of an electron—myopic and self-centered.) Other evidence of perceptual narrowness appears in the *History of Shikasta*, where we learn that even during earth's greatest crisis, the period between World War II and III, the "Shikastan compartmentalism of mind reigned supreme, almost unchallenged—except by [Canopean] servants and agents, continually at work trying to restore balances, and to heal these woeful defects of imaginative understanding" (349). In this description of the work of Canopean agents Lessing seems to suggest her own artistic intentions in writing these novels, as she too is bent on overcoming the compartmentalism that threatens to destroy us all.

Johor himself is sent to Shikasta originally to help it overcome the effects of the "Degenerative Disease." This is defined as the desire "to identify with ourselves as individuals"—a weakness that first struck the planet's native population in the Time of the Catastrophe (38). As a Canopean envoy, Johor must take the responsibility during his first visit to remind the inhabitants that we are "all creatures of the stars and their forces, they make us, we make them, we are part of a dance from which we by no means and not ever may consider ourselves separate" (40)—a message hauntingly close to that delivered by Charles Watkins in *Briefing for a Descent into Hell*. But when Johor arrives he finds that even the Giants show symptoms of the Degenerative Disease. Theirs is a particularly critical falling away for, as we have seen, they are tutors to the Shikastans. It is also the Giants who have built the cities and aligned the stones that have provided the patterns necessary for the Lock between Shikasta and Canopus.[18]

The origins of the Degenerative Disease are literally in a "*disaster*"; that is, "a fault in the stars" that has disturbed the "stellar alignments" and left vulnerable the planet that was originally known as Rohanda, "which means fruitful, thriving" (21, 15; Lessing's emphasis). Because the cosmic patterns have been realigned, the planet has been left weakened, susceptible to the ravages of the disease introduced by Shammat, the empire of evil and corruption. When Johor tries to explain to the Giants that "Shammat cannot feed on the high, the pure, the fine," he finds them incapable of understanding the concept of an enemy (44). He attributes this blindness to the fact that they are constitutionally not "able to credit the reality of types of mind keyed to theft and destruction" (22). In other words, as wise and intelligent as they are, they too are limited by their own perspective, by their own "benign and nurturing minds" (22).

When Johor finally accepts the fact that the Giants have fundamentally changed, he turns to two natives, David and Sais, to help him spread the word of Canopus throughout what is no longer Rohanda but Shikasta, "the hurt, the damaged, the wounded one" (24). As things fall apart, Johor moves quickly to warn the natives of impending catastrophe. His problem is complicated by the fact that they "had not been programmed for failure, disaster" (49). To comfort them, he tells them that Shikasta is to receive "a small steady trickle" of substance-of-we-feeling (73). He is able to keep the attention of the natives for as long as he does, only because he places in front of them what he calls the Signature, a device that subconsciously recalls to their minds the existence of Canopus. When Johor leaves the Signature with Sais, he is in effect transferring his authority to her (which makes for a nice literary touch to Lessing's metaphor, as a "signature" is the term for the printer's notations that indicate how a book is to be assembled and Johor clearly is the informing consciousness of this novel).

If Johor is the novel's authorial voice (even though his and Lessing's ideas do not always coincide), Rachel Sherban is its naive narrator. As such, she represents the viewpoint that would be shared by Lessing's readers if it were not for the fact that Johor had already won us over to Lessing's alternative historical paradigms. Rachel Sherban is a bright young woman, who, by writing a diary, is trying to sort out the mystery of her enigmatic, influential brother, George Sherban, whom we know already as Johor. Not only is she unaware that he is a Canopean envoy, but she has apparently never even heard of Canopus. What she records of George therefore is based only on her severely limited knowledge of him in his human guise. When she describes the reaction of complete strangers to him, for example, she is puzzled both by their sudden desire to take him on as a student and by her parents' inexplicable willingness to let them do so. Similarly, when she listens to George talk with his friends, she knows that they are saying more than she can catch, but she never really understands what it is. "I could see from George's face," she writes, "that in quite ordinary things that were said was much much more. I just couldn't grasp it" (226). As readers, however, we know what is going on in these instances because we have read Johor's narrative in part one. We know, for example, that he is being sought out by other emissaries or by people who are still in touch with the substance-of-we-feeling flowing from Canopus to Shikasta. They seek him out because they recognize his true identity and want to help him "develop quickly . . . without incapacitating damage" (203). We know further that the subtext of George's conversation is based on the

Canopean philosophy of wholeness and the need to recover it as soon as possible. In other words, by reading more into Rachel's account than she knows is there, we acknowledge our acceptance of Lessing's point of view. Without the ironic distance here that is set up by Johor's narration in part one, we would not be able to separate ourselves from Rachel's viewpoint in part two because it is so very like our own otherwise would be.

What we encounter in reading Rachel's journal is a kind of intra-textual recognition as she, albeit unknowingly, gives us information about Johor that has been, through her human perspective, totally defamiliarized. What Johor reports to Canopus may be a defamiliarized version of known reality, but what Rachel reports about George is a defamiliarized version of alien reality—a reality that Johor himself introduced us to. When Rachel quotes George as saying "this is a terrible place," she reports that upon reflection she "saw that he was not talking about Nigeria" (213).[19] Although she may not know enough to understand what George means, we know. When George tells her that if she cannot handle the pain, she will "have to come back and do it all over again, " we know that he is referring to the fact that while they were both in Zone Six he encouraged her to submit herself to reincarnation in the hopes of finally earning an end to the painful process of rebirth (270). There she was known as Rilla, an identity she seems not to recall while she is Rachel Sherban.

As these passages suggest, Rachel's journal is juxtaposed to Johor's report to contrast the human and alien points of view—a contrast that is provided by other documents as well. Juxtaposed to her innocent account of the pending holocaust, for example, are reports from both Shammatan and Sirian agents. Of the period Rachel writes, "So much is happening all the time and I can't grasp it" (265). Like other human beings she is unaware of the fact that, ever since the Lock was weakened between earth and Canopus, Shammat has been actively participating in world affairs in order to accelerate a large-scale disaster on which it will feed. Those humans who guess the truth are either dismissed or punished by their superiors for speaking out. Although Rachel remains ignorant of this information, we are privy to it from the reports of Tafta, the Shammatan agent. In his transmission to the Supreme Supervisory Lord Zarlem, he describes how Shammat has disrupted life on Shikasta simply by instructing various leaders to speak honestly about the crisis, proving in the process that "the planet is immune to truth" (262). If Shammat revels in the disorder, Sirius does not, fearing as it does for the safety of its colonies. The Sirian agent, Ambien II, reports that the Shammatans on Shikasta are suffering from "hectivity, acceleration, arrhythmictivity," a condition she thinks "likely to add to the spontaneous and random destructivity to be expected of Shikasta at this time" (265; this passage is quoted in full in *The Sirian Experiments*, making for another clear-cut example of inter-textual recognition). Quite unexpectedly, the reports from Tafta and Ambien II carry more weight in our imaginations than the uninformed descriptions in Rachel's journal. It is as though what these two aliens report is more true than what Rachel reports. In short, by the time we get to this part of the novel, we have accepted the alien perspective as the normative perspective and begun to question the human perspective for being too limited.

If it is important for us to have a complete understanding of Canopus when we read Rachel's journal, it is equally important when we read the letters and reports written by Chen Liu, the Chinese Overlord "in charge of the People's Secret Services, Europe" (264). As a naive narrator, Rachel is truly ingenuous; in contrast, Chen Liu is utterly disingenuous. Where she represents the limitations of anthropocentric perspectives, he represents the extent of human corruption. He represents, in fact, the highest political authority on earth at the time of Johor's final visit. But just as Lessing undermined the authority of Charles Watkins's doctors, she undermines the authority of this overlord who parrots the party line. She does this primarily by counterpointing the rhetoric, philosophy, and activities of the Canopean Empire with those of the Chinese Empire. Both profess to operate out of the high-minded ideals of beneficent centralized government. But it is clear that of the two, only Canopus truly acts in the interests of its citizens; the Chinese government acts in its own self-interest. Both may be colonizers of the northern hemisphere, but only Canopus improves the lives of its colonized citizens; the Chinese government uses these people for its own glorification and punishes them unmercifully when they do not obey.

In addition to countering the claims made on behalf of his government by Chen Liu, Lessing also throws in an unexpected development. Although Chen Liu tries to convince his superiors—and in the process himself—that he strictly adheres to the official government dogma, he slowly but surely becomes converted to George's point of view. The last we learn of him appears in a note from the Archivists to the effect that he and his friend Ku Yuang "were sequestered, and underwent 'beneficent correction' until their deaths" (341). Like so much of Lessing's work, this passage serves to warn us once again how ruthlessly intolerant and self-serving are any and all totalitarian states. But it also reminds us, on a more positive note, that the most hopelessly intransigent individuals can be reformed by the right kind of persuasion.

As the above discussion suggests, Lessing's purpose in dividing her book into two sections appears to be twofold. In the first place, she divides it in order to help insure credibility for her account of the apostasy, destruction, and redemption of the world. That is, in part one, Lessing establishes the reality base of her novel, a reality that at nearly every point, as we have seen, contradicts what we believe to be true of life on earth. In part two, this unconventional, alien perspective is challenged—if only indirectly—by the human perspective of Rachel Sherban and Chen Liu, neither of whom know anything at all about Canopus or its envoys. Because these two mortals express our own sense of reality, we might expect their narration to undermine the credibility of Johor's reports. But this does not occur, as we continue to regard his account as more "real" than theirs. We maintain our epistemological allegiance to Johor primarily because his perception of reality continues to dominate the book. In other words, Rachel and Chen Liu express views that are valid outside the text but not inside it. Because of the way the novel has been constructed, an ironic distance is set up between these two human beings and us, a distance that discourages us from believing them.

In terms of Lessing's alien cosmology, which Johor has completely and compellingly described, therefore, Rachel is a naive narrator who cannot gain our trust for the simple reason that we know more than she does. The Chinese Overlord is even less trustworthy because he represents a totalitarian government that is trying to impede George's work. In short, what Lessing does, by presenting her alternative cosmology at the beginning of the text, is to insure its credibility throughout the text. When she presents evidence in part two that purportedly would contradict the particulars of her cosmology, we are not dissuaded. Instead, we are further disarmed by the presence of contradictory evidence. Our seduction is further assured by the fact that, although we do not believe Rachel, we like her. That is, under normal circumstances, we would want to believe her view of events. So when we choose here not to believe her, the choice strengthens our belief in Johor's alternative reality.

And yet, if it is important to Lessing's purpose that she establish a new definition of reality and a new interpretation of human history, it is also important that she does not corral her readers into just another closed system of thought. So if she structures her novel to give more credibility to ideas that run counter to conventional reality or official explanations, she must be wary of replacing one form of authority with another (however superior it might appear to be). To help prevent this from happening, she includes the conventional viewpoints of an ordinary citizen and those of a government official. Thus, although she stacks the deck in favor of our accepting Johor's ideas, she does provide us with alternatives to them. This then is the other reason she has divided her book into two parts. By including these conflicting points of view in part two, Lessing maintains a reasonably open text through which she allows her readers the freedom to decide for themselves where they will stand on the issues she raises.

Because her position, as expressed by Johor, is so radically different from ours, Lessing must give credence to these ideas by providing them with more narrative support than is needed by the conventional ideas expressed by Rachel and Chen Liu. Without this extra narrative reinforcement, the temptation on our part would be to dismiss her ideas as fanciful nonsense with little accompanying thought for their validity or importance. With the reinforcement she maintains the tension (the dialectic) she needs to get our attention and stimulate thought and debate. Thus the two-part structure of her novel serves to establish two convincing poles of a dialectic. And the dialectics found in the novel's extensive defamiliarization serve to reinforce this one, until we are left at the end with a world that has been transformed before our very eyes. Although Shikasta is destroyed by nuclear war, Johor/George's people are there to pick up the pieces and create what promises to be a better place to live. And, if Lessing's text has been successful, so it is with us. Although our comfortable, conventional worldview has been subverted by the text, we too have a glimmer of hope that

indeed the universe is a "roaring engine of creativity." Thus it is
that out of opposition Lessing has forged her utopian vision of the
future, where there will be abundant substance-of-we-feeling to
carry us through what promises to be a never-ending process of
change.

NOTES

1. At this point, it is unclear whether additional volumes are forthcoming
or not.

2. For additional insight into this revolution of ideas, see Thomas S.
Kuhn, *The Copernican Revolution: Planetary Astronomy in the
Development of Western Thought* (1957; rpt. Cambridge: Harvard
University Press, 1975); and Owen Barfield, *Saving the Appearances: A
Study in Idolatry* (New York: Harcourt, Brace & World, 1965), especially
his chapter "Appearance and Hypothesis," in which he reminds us that
hypotheses were originally "arrangements—devices—for saving the
appearances; and the Greek and medieval astronomers were not at all
disturbed by the fact that the same appearances could be saved by two or
more quite different hypotheses" (49). Thus, Barfield notes, the "real
turning-point in the history of astronomy and of science in
general . . . took place when Copernicus . . . began to affirm that the
heliocentric hypothesis not only saved the appearances, but was physically
true" (50). In short, what had before been regarded simply as models
became (and remain) in our imagination indistinguishable from truth. For
more on this, see chapter 7 below.

3. Doris Lessing, "Preface" to *The Sirian Experiments* (New York:
Alfred A. Knopf, 1980), viii.

4. For a discussion of this, see Betsy Draine, *Substance Under Pressure:
Artistic Coherence and Evolving Form in the Novels of Doris Lessing*
(Madison: University of Wisconsin Press, 1983), 106-10.

5. Doris Lessing, "Some Remarks," preface to *Re: Colonised Planet 5,
Shikasta* (New York: Alfred A. Knopf, 1979), ix. Subsequent page
references appear in the text. A note on the title. There are three different
versions of this title: *Shikasta* is the shortest and most frequently used version; what I have used above is the mid-length version; the full title is *Re:
Colonised Planet 5, Shikasta: Personal, Psychological, Historical Documents Relating to Visit by JOHOR (George Sherban), Emissary (Grade 9)
87th of the Period of the Last Days*. Because it is part of a series,
technically, even this title should be preceded by *Canopus in Argos:
Archives*—as should all subsequent novels in the series. For the sake of
brevity, I have not included this phrase in my citations.

6. For a general discussion of this subject, see Tom Kitwood, " 'Science' and 'Utopia' in the Marxist Tradition," *Alternative Futures: The Journal of Utopian Studies*, 1, no. 2 (Summer 1978), 24-46.

7. "Report on the Threatened City" was first published in *Playboy* magazine in November 1971. It is collected in Doris Lessing, *The Temptation of Jack Orkney and Other Stories* (1972; rpt. New York: Bantam Books, 1974), 79-117. For a discussion of the relationship between *Shikasta* and *Last and First Men*, see Betsy Draine, *Substance Under Pressure*, 147. For a discussion of what happens to her thinking when she reads this story, see Judith Stitzel, "Reading Doris Lessing," *College English*, 40, no. 5 (January 1979), 498-504.

8. By a rhetorical text I mean a text that points us self-consciously to its own construction and in so doing points us outside the text. It is comparable to Sheldon Sacks's "apologue," which he defines in "Golden Birds and Dying Generations," *Comparative Literature Studies*, 6, no. 3 (September 1969), 277. For more on this, see the introduction above.

9. Doris Lessing, *The Golden Notebook* (1962; rpt. New York: Bantam Books, 1973), 63.

10. Doris Lessing, *Briefing for a Descent into Hell* (New York: Alfred A. Knopf, 1971), 17. Subsequent page references appear in the text.

11. The correspondence between these novels can be used to argue, as I have done elsewhere, that, contrary to the thinking of some critics, *Briefing for a Descent into Hell* is science fiction—in part because it anticipates so many of the images, devices, and ideas that are found throughout *Canopus in Argos*.

12. Doris Lessing, "The Temptation of Jack Orkney," in *The Temptation of Jack Orkney and Other Stories*, 274-75.

13. For more on this, see the discussion on Tom Kitwood's " 'Science' and 'Utopia' in the Marxist Tradition" found in the introduction above.

14. The defamiliarization works so well in taking us out of the realm of the ordinary that, earlier in the text, when the phrase "World War II" is used (p. 76), we are struck by its inappropriateness to the alien context that has been established.

15. In a recent interview with Lesley Hazleton, Lessing does however suggest that nuclear war might very well be inevitable and, rather than trying to prevent it, we might better spend our time preparing to survive it ("Doris Lessing on Feminism, Communism, and 'Space Fiction,' " *New York Times Magazine*, 25 July 1982, p. 28). See also chapter 6 below.

16. In the interview with Lesley Hazleton (cited above), Lessing also addresses the question of evolution under stress. See also chapter 6 below.

17. In this respect her fiction resembles such post-holocaust utopian fiction as Suzy McKee Charnas's *Motherlines*, where the holocaust is portrayed as the ultimate agent of women's liberation, capable of

undermining our entire sexist society and returning small groups of free women to life in the wilderness without men (1978; rpt. New York: Berkley, 1979). Lessing's attitude toward the holocaust can also be compared to Thea Alexander's in the latter's apology for "macro" philosophy—the utopian novel *2150 A.D.* (New York: Warner Books, 1976). In this novel Alexander asserts that "Micro man had to perish so that Macro man could be born. Death is only bad when it is taken out of the context of the soul evolution and the cumulative Macro effect" (190). See also chapter 6 below.

18. Lessing has remarked in another recent interview that she wonders "if buildings affect the mentality of people in ways we haven't begun to research. This is my thought. This is my specific thought, not metaphorical . . . . I think it will turn out that there is a whole science of building that we know nothing about, that we might have lost and that ancient civilizations might have known about" (Minda Bikman, "A Talk With Doris Lessing," *New York Times Book Review*, 30 March 1980, p. 26). In these ideas Lessing also reflects those of the religious historian Mircea Eliade, who notes that "to organize a space is to repeat the paradigmatic work of the gods," making space meaningful and sacred (*The Sacred and the Profane: The Nature of Religion*, trans. Willard R. Trask, 1957; rpt. New York: Harcourt, Brace & World, 1959), 32.

19. This is exactly what a Canopean agent says about earth in *The Sirian Experiments*: " 'This is a terrible place,' he said in a bleak voice, as if suddenly seeing something for the first time—he who had lived with this for so long! Yet he was contemplating it again, anew. 'A terrible place' " (144).

4.

The Dialectic of Sex: *The Marriages Between Zones Three, Four, and Five*

If some of her readers had been disgruntled to learn that Shikasta was to be but the first of many novels in a new science fiction series by Doris Lessing, they were no doubt somewhat mollified by the unexpected direction this series took in *The Marriages Between Zones Three, Four, and Five* (1980).[1] Not only does the second novel give us characters we can relate to, but it also introduces us to a new story in a new setting without making any specific reference to Shikastans or Shikasta. At the same time, it places Lessing's Canopean machinery more in the background, where it can inform the novel without dominating it. As I suggested earlier, the narrative differences between these first two novels are indicative of the kinds of differences that mark this entire series. Although all five of these novels have much in common, each one does tell a separate story.[2] As a series they also provide five experimental variations on Lessing's major ideas—ideas that focus primarily on the need to transform our view of the world. In their own narrative differences, therefore, they suggest the very activity that Lessing would invite us to emulate—that being a continual questioning of the world in which we live.

Unlike *Shikasta*, which is in the documentary or political tradition characteristic of Olaf Stapledon and John Brunner, *Marriages* is in the romantic or fantastic tradition of David Lindsay, Dorothy Bryant, and Marion Zimmer Bradley. *Shikasta*, in other words, is a richly woven tapestry that takes as its subject matter most of Western history, while *Marriages* is its domestic counterpart, a less ambitious but brilliantly conceived miniature—a utopian fabulation.[3] But even with its narrower focus, it is still intellectually and emotionally satisfying. In part it is satisfying because it holds out the hope that the world can redeem itself without having to experience the agony of global destruction. In its hopeful message and almost bucolic setting, in which war itself has been reduced to little more than men's games, *Marriages* offers us a brief but effective respite from the depressing scenarios mapped out for us previously in *Shikasta* (not to mention Lessing's other science fiction). Given its lighter flavor, it is possible that one of its functions is to help us persevere during a long and difficult series. One way it helps us keep going is by reducing the scope of Lessing's subject, by giving us something with which we can more readily identify. Although the metaphor of social conflict and change Lessing has chosen here, that of a marriage, is a humbler example than we are accustomed to finding in her science fiction, it is no less convincing a statement of her position. Perhaps, like John Hersey's masterpiece of understatement, *Hiroshima*, it is even more convincing. For rather than witnessing a panoramic view of the decline of civilization as we do in *Shikasta*, here we observe, with much less sense of helplessness and considerably more sympathy, the struggles of two people to change their view of the world and in so doing help to save it. Instead of being overwhelmed by the horrors of it all, here we are given some hope that individual action can make a difference.

The novel is narrated by an officially appointed chronicler of Zone Three, who, like Lessing herself, works from the knowledge that his audience will resist and even resent his call for change. For the world Lusik describes is a virtual utopia which only recently has been faced with disaster—the prospects of universal infertility. The apparent cause of this infertility is Zone Three's long-lasting and hurtful isolation from the two zones that border it. Especially hurtful to its chances for growth has been its isolation from the much more bellicose and untamed world of Zone Four. As far as anyone can remember, these two zones have never mingled and are widely reputed to be "inimical by nature."[4] Moreover, Zone Three considers itself so superior to its less sophisticated neighbors that over time it has virtually forgotten that they exist. In an effort to correct this situation, a mysterious outside force known only as the Providers orders Al•Ith, the queen of Zone Three, to marry Ben Ata, the king of Zone Four.[5] Because of the division between these two zones, the people of Zone Three are shocked and not a little offended to be forced into communication with what they consider to be an inferior, unruly people.

Although Lessing does not describe the consequences of the two zones' isolation in the apocalyptic terms she uses elsewhere, she does suggest in her basic metaphor of marriage that serious consequences will befall these people if they do not change immediately. That is, she strongly implies that if the zones do not initiate meaningful contact and stop seeing themselves in such narrowly chauvinistic terms, the birthrate will fall until it reaches the point of no return. While this would, of course, be catastrophic were it to happen to any group, a steadily declining birthrate does not have quite the dramatic impact of, say, a nuclear war. But it is a threat calculated to fit the situation. Just as Lessing portrays the outbreak of war on the technologically glutted Shikasta, she portrays the waning of desire in the three zones that are crippled by self-satisfaction and isolationism. And what more appropriate punishment is there for a world dedicated to the perpetuation of the status quo than to threaten it with absolute stagnation—the promise that no future generation will bring unwanted change for the simple reason that there will be no future generation? To help prevent this eventuality, which both know from recent experience to be a real threat to their zones, Al•Ith and Ben Ata must assume the lead for their people by establishing social and intellectual intercourse among them.

This solution, like so many in Lessing's fiction, hinges on a paradox in that it makes a virtue out of the potential for conflict between unfriendly nations. In *Shikasta*, it will be recalled, Lessing uses the device of recognition to demonstrate that the major powers of the twentieth century have consistently invoked the myth of their national differences to camouflage their virtually indistinguishable imperialistic actions—actions that threaten the very existence of the world itself. She argues her point, moreover, in passages that clearly refer to defamiliarized versions of specific, recognizable countries. In *Marriages*, on the other hand, although she poses dialectical relationships between the zones, she does not identify any one zone with a particular world power in the real world. Instead, she defamiliarizes the idea of conflict itself. But in a kind of Marxian turnabout, she affirms here—just as she did in *Shikasta*—the role of conflict in social progress. In *Marriages*, therefore, we again encounter the apparently paradoxical situation where political conflict is both bad and good. It is bad if it originates in fear and misunderstanding and perpetuates the kind of divisiveness that leads to war. (Here Lessing deviates from revolutionary Marxism, as she does not believe in the necessity of armed rebellion, although she often predicts the accidental outbreak of war.) Political conflict is good, on the other hand, if it can be used to rejuvenate worn-out societies that are suffering from a lack of fresh ideas and a reluctance to change. In her utopian vision, therefore, the very dialectic that at the beginning threatens to destroy Zones Three and Four becomes the same process that they need to experience in order to grow, to change. It is the same dialectic that helps us to a new vision of wholeness, as the recognition we experience in reading about their conflict leads us to a re-cognition in which we assimilate both poles of the argument.

For it is primarily in the conflict itself—in the differing perspectives of Zones Three and Four especially—that we encounter most of the novel's recognition, as throughout the text we are asked to look anew at familiar problems. Thus it is that, while we do not recognize either Zone Three or Four as being a displaced version of any particular country we know, we do recognize the attitudes that keep them apart and fearful of one another. We also recognize that behind their political differences lies the same dangerous nationalism characteristic of current world powers. Finally, we recognize that, although both zones make virtues of their differences, both behave alike in that neither wants to have any dealings with the other and neither wants to disturb the status quo. (Not insignificantly, the only exception to this rule is the attitude of the women of Zone Four—as they very much long for contact with Zone Three.) As a result of the blind nationalistic drives they share, both zones also share the same life-threatening problem of a seriously endangered birthrate. In short we recognize in Lessing's metaphors the same self-destructive tendencies that threaten to engulf us all in war.

But even though we recognize problems that are familiar to us from Lessing's earlier science fiction, she has added an unexpected twist to her metaphor in this novel. In her first three novels, as we have seen, Lessing defamiliarizes the major political, scientific, and religious institutions of everyday life in order to call them to our attention—and condemn them. In *Briefing*, for example, by portraying society as a mental hospital, she suggests just how fouled up and rigidly authoritarian most social institutions are. The only way to escape the confines of a mad society, she implies here, is to escape from reality itself. In *Memoirs* she describes how the collapse of civilization results from technological irresponsibility and the failure of governments to meet the needs of their people. Again she implies that the only solution is to leave this world of officially sanctioned corruption. In *Shikasta* she blames all our major institutions for the devastation of the planet, implying that our only salvation lies in their complete reformation or outright destruction. In *Marriages*, on the other hand, she demonstrates how one very common social institution, that of an arranged yet fairly conventional marriage, can be liberating and enriching to the individuals involved and to society at large.[6]

This marriage is beneficial to society because Al•Ith and Ben Ata are more than just individuals; they are symbols of their two zones. Theirs is not only a marriage between two individuals, therefore, but also a marriage between two ways of life. It is the conjunction of thesis and antithesis: it is the dialectic of sex as described by Shulamith Firestone in her book of that name.[7] In this controversial analysis, Firestone argues that all our current social problems have originated in the biological division between human males and females. Although she would agree that the biological distinction between the sexes is both natural and genetically necessary for the well-being of the species, she contends that the social distinctions that have arisen out of it are neither natural nor necessary. To the contrary, by rigidly dividing the world against itself, these distinctions have always been harmful to both sexes—and, in a nuclear age, have become a threat to our very existence as a planet. For in this division, according to Firestone, women have been assigned one set of qualities and men another—assignments that generally disadvantage women and keep them and their children in subordinate and powerless positions while purporting to elevate them. In this sexual dichotomy, women have been relegated to the aesthetic or ideal mode and men the technological or pragmatic mode, with little crossover expected of men or permitted of women. By separating the moral arena (dominated by women) from the technological arena (dominated by men), human society has, in Firestone's view, practically guaranteed its own destruction. Although Lessing's description of society is not identical to Firestone's she too is setting up a dialectic based on the differences traditionally used to divide the sexes into separate spheres of experience and influence.

In Zone Three, for example, all persons live in harmony with nature and are able to communicate with animals—a closeness usually ascribed to women which forms the background of much recent feminist science fiction, such as Sally Miller Gearhart's *The Wanderground* (1979) and Suzy McKee Charnas's *Motherlines* (1978). In keeping with another pattern in feminist science fiction, such as that found in Marge Piercy's *Woman on the Edge of Time* (1976) and Vonda N. McIntyre's *Dreamsnake* (1978), the sexual codes of Zone Three are more relaxed and egalitarian than those of the sexually repressive Zone Four. Similarly, the responsibilities for childbearing and rearing are shared by both sexes in Zone Three, while in Zone Four they remain entirely women's business. Because Zone Three has no armies and fights no wars, its people have been able to redirect their science and technology along the life-affirming lines suggested by Herbert Marcuse in *An Essay on Liberation.*[8] As a result, these people are free from want and from war. This is in direct contrast to what takes place in Zone Four, where the people are continually impoverished because their government spends all its wealth on its standing armies. Although Lessing herself comes close to reaffirming sexual stereotypes in characterizing these two zones as quintessentially male and female, she does avoid the pitfall in her description of the queen of Zone Five. After presenting us with the almost overly refined Al•Ith, Lessing gives us in Vahshi an untamed woman warrior in the tradition of Karrakaz, the heroine of Tanith Lee's *The Birthgrave* (1975), or Rifkind, the heroine of Lynn Abbey's *Daughter of the Bright Moon* (1979). In another turnabout, by the end of Lessing's novel, it is Ben Ata, the former bully and ruffian, who faces the task of civilizing Vahshi, who comes from a zone where war is "a way of life" (210). In her portrait of this warrior queen, therefore, Lessing has given us the antithesis to the gentle peace-loving example of Al•Ith and thus increased the complexity of her dialectics.[9]

The differences between Al•Ith and Ben Ata are most notable when the two have sexual intercourse together. In fact, from the way that Lessing emphasizes it throughout the novel, it is clear that the sex act itself constitutes the heart of her marital metaphor. With Al•Ith, as might be expected, sex is all subtle nuances and choreographed pleasures based on an intimate knowledge of the body. With Ben Ata, sex is an act of aggression, a show of power he wields over the women his soldiers capture for him. In their first sexual encounter on their wedding night, Ben Ata prevails and rapes his bride. It is only later, when they have made a real effort to communicate, that the sex between them is good and the relationship matures—developments the Providers reward by letting them stay together. When things go poorly, Ben Ata reverts to old habits of sexual violence and abuses Al•Ith—behavior the Providers punish by separating them. Sex is central to Lessing's metaphor in this novel because the underlying purpose of the marriage between Al•Ith and Ben Ata is to stimulate procreation among their people. Literally, this procreation takes the form of an increased birthrate; figuratively, it takes the form of intellectual growth and change, a change that can only occur when the zones interact with one another, a change that is *given birth to* by conflict and communion.

For their marriage to work, Al•Ith and Ben Ata must learn to communicate with sympathy and mutual understanding, a communion that involves both sex and conversation.[10] Their initial failure to communicate is symbolized by Ben Ata's sexual violence to which Al•Ith passively submits on their wedding night. In this degrading behavior both feel that they are doing their duty in consummating a marriage that neither wants. But the consummation is hardly successful as it brings neither one any pleasure, and it does not lead to conception. In short, it is not what the Providers had in mind at all. It is more what they are trying to eliminate in the two zones. Because of Al•Ith and Ben Ata's uncooperative attitude, the Providers send Al•Ith back to her own zone where she is expected to come to terms with her new responsibility, just as Ben Ata is to

come to terms with his. At this point in their relationship, the two behave as though they are in combat, thus transforming Lessing's
marital metaphor into a martial metaphor. But in their unwilling-
ness to get along, Al•Ith and Ben Ata simply reflect the animosity
of their two zones. In their reluctance to consummate their marriage,
they also reflect the infertility plaguing their zones, as each confesses to the other that their worlds "have lost the will to mate"
(41). Because both are "representatives and *embodiments* of their
respective countries," what they do together out of bed as well as in
will help determine the future of their people (45; my emphasis).[11]
If they are to improve the fertility of their lands, these two rulers
must do more than go through the motions of a marriage. It is only
when they truly marry, in the full sexual sense of knowing one
another, therefore, that they are able to perform the sympathetic
magic needed by their worlds.

If this union is to be described accurately as one with the
potential for "fusing the imaginations of two realms," it must be
based on mutual trust, respect, and a willingness to change (35). As
we have seen, on their wedding night it is duty, and not desire, that
drives Ben Ata to rape Al•Ith—just as it is duty that forces her to
submit to him without resistance. But even though both resist the
idea of this marriage, the first night they spend together does begin
to change them. Ben Ata, for example, decides that as alien as her
ways are to him, he still wants to "understand" her better (38).
When he virtually rapes her again in the morning, he feels her
flinch and can only keep going by "taking a furtive glance at the
bruise he had inflicted"—an act that fills him with shame and grief
(46). If Ben Ata is learning to be more sensitive to the needs of
women, Al•Ith is learning humility, forced as she is into the role of
victim on her wedding night. This experience shocks her because it
is so foreign to what she has known as a woman in the more utopian Zone Three, where everyone is treated with respect and loving
attention.

As she journeys home under the Providers' orders, she sees
further changes in herself that lead her to mourn the passing of the
person she has been. Thinking of Ben Ata, she realizes that he
represents a "descent into possibilities of herself she had not
believed open to her" (58). Although she longs to avoid these
changes, she knows intuitively that they will be beneficial to her-

self and her people. Nonetheless she is plagued by "calamitous and heavy emotions," which she only gradually comes to identify as guilt, meaning that she, Al•Ith, is somehow to blame for the problems faced by her people (58). What makes her realization so long in coming is "the knowledge, which was the base of all knowledges, that everything was entwined and mixed and mingled, all was one, that there was no such thing as an individual in the wrong, nor could there be" (58). If she has behaved incorrectly, therefore, so has everyone else. With this she realizes that she herself has managed to forget all about Zones One and Two. Shaken by her feelings that Zone Two represents "some very strong and urgent need" that she must address, she stops to gaze into its "long, blue deceiving distances" (59). In so doing, she sees for the first time that somehow her new husband "must balance in some way those far blue heights" (61).

While Al•Ith is making these discoveries about the source of her zone's malaise and her own part in its continuance, Ben Ata has been making some discoveries of his own. Although the division between them is not exact, those changes first undergone by Al•Ith are primarily spiritual or psychological and those by Ben Ata primarily physical or pragmatic—a division parallel to that established by Shulamith Firestone. But the more each one changes, the more each begins to resemble the other. That is, the connection Al•Ith sees between her marriage to Ben Ata and the mysteries of Zone Two suggests that she knows, if only tacitly, that she and he are engaged in a celebration of the world's oneness—a oneness based not on the dissolution of differences but on their affirmation and integration. This awareness marks the beginning of a spiritual journey that eventually leads her into the hidden summits of Zone Two, a journey that takes her out of the realm of the physical and into the realm of the mystical.

In the meantime, Ben Ata's initial response to his marriage is to learn how to enjoy sex more. At this point he is only concerned with increasing his physical pleasure, but even this thoroughly pragmatic response eventually leads him to more profound psychological changes. While Al•Ith is away, he comes to the discovery that he does not know much about the art of making love. To correct this lack, he makes "methodical enquiries" of his men and finds a skilled courtesan to instruct him (67). Although it might be tempting to shrug—or laugh—off Ben Ata's actions as inferior to Al•Ith's, to do so would be to misread the text, which, as I have already indicated, continually emphasizes the importance of the sex act itself in suggesting the success or failure of the marriage. In other words, if Ben Ata and Al•Ith are to understand one another, even their bodies must learn to communicate with one another. Through this metaphor, Lessing affirms Michael Polanyi's belief that all we know of the outside world comes to us through our bodies' interaction with it—that our bodies are the instruments "of all our external knowledge, whether intellectual or practical."[12] Because of Ben Ata's lessons from the courtesan, when he and Al•Ith meet again she is able to "teach him how to be equal and ready in love," an instruction that leaves him open to strange new emotions (68). No longer compelled to rape her, he finds himself instead "engulfed in tenderness, in passion, in the wildest intensities that he did not know whether to call pain or delight" (68). At this moment they become "entirely and thoroughly wedded" (68). In this physical union, they accomplish the purpose of the marriage—an accomplishment symbolized by the steady beat of a drum and the fact of Al•Ith's pregnancy.

Nor do their changes end with the conception of their child. Before the marriage is dissolved by the Providers and superceded by Ben Ata's marriage to Vahshi, both he and Al•Ith undergo significant transformations in their view of the world. Al•Ith's changes are perhaps the more interesting of the two as they are signified by specific changes in her body—not the least of which is the pregnancy itself. When she arrives from Zone Three, for example, she is all lightness and grace. But the longer she stays married to Ben Ata, the more her body grows to resemble Zone Four, in part because of her pregnancy and in part because she is acclimating herself to her new environment. When she returns home for a visit to Zone Three, one of her former sexual partners tells her that it appears as though her body had assumed "a new substance" (112). Her transformation is so complete that this formerly popular queen is able to walk among her former subjects without being recognized. What has happened, of course, is that Al•Ith has become more like Ben Ata at the same time he has become more like her. As he had when she first met him, now she too expresses in herself and her body the "nature of Zone Four," which is one of "conflict and battle and warring'' (114). When she returns to Zone Four, therefore, she finds that she ''no longer considered the products of this land as impossible to her'' (128). Shortly afterward she also realizes that she loves Ben Ata ''utterly,'' a discovery that binds her more closely to the women of Zone Four than she had previously thought possible (144). The bond is reinforced when the women attend her in childbirth, an event that leaves her looking ''heavy, lightless, even coarse'' (166). Significantly, these changes extend to her sexual behavior, which has become both supplicating and aggressive, horrifying her husband who had learned to delight in her playful and self-assured sexuality.

Just as Al•Ith learns to accept Ben Ata's world as her own, he learns to see it through her eyes. He begins to see, for example, that his people have suffered because of his obsession with warfare. Traveling throughout the very poorest part of his lands, he is shocked by its poverty and sends his men home to rebuild the country more in keeping with the ideals of Zone Three. At the same time he realizes that he can no longer see the people of Zone Three as enemies, nor can he see himself as a soldier; he is in fact deeply divided about who he is and what he should be doing. Aware that his own transformation has resulted from Al•Ith's influence, he overturns the rule against ''cloud-gathering'' that had prevented his people from gazing into the hills of Zone Three. In fact, it soon becomes common knowledge that he is setting a new example for his people by ''teaching his son to look upwards'' toward the mountains of his mother (218). And because his sexual behavior is always indicative of his state of mind, he is no longer able to take a woman ''as he had always in the past, without thought for her, not considering her as an individual creature'' (160). In sum, where Al•Ith has given birth to the messianic child who would ''in some way redeem them all, and through them, the kingdom as a whole,'' Ben Ata gives birth in himself to a new wisdom (165).

Out of the changed perspective given him by Al•Ith, Ben Ata, in turn, is able to help Vahshi expand her horizons. When he first encounters her, for example, he watches himself ''with an eye which he knew was Al•Ith's—or at least, was her gift to him'' (209). And as his relationship with his new wife develops, he acknowledges that ''he was for ever caught up and bound, if not to Al•Ith, then to her realm, her ways—so that he could never act without thinking, or be without reflection on his condition'' (211). As a result of this marriage, Vahshi herself is changed profoundly and feels ''set apart from the life of her people, and responsible in a way she did not understand'' (217). As the Providers had intended, the marriages' beneficial influences also spread to the zones themselves where there is among them now ''a continuous movement'' and a ''remaking and an inspiration where there had been only stagnation'' (244, 245).

If the contributions of Al•Ith and Ben Ata are essential to bringing this change into their zones, so too are the contributions of the songmakers, painters, and chroniclers. Without the efforts of these artists, the marriages that take place would have remained nothing more than symbolic gestures of unification among the zones. Because the people in their isolation had become so chauvinistic in their view of other zones, they receive the news of the two marriages with outrage. It is only because of the interpretive endeavors of the artists that these marriages become meaningful, instructive events in the lives of the general populace. What the artists do, in other words, is to help the people see what the marriages mean to the three zones. But before the artists can help heal the schism between the zones, much like Lessing herself they must first reflect their differences.

The kinds of songs that are found in the two zones help to suggest the differences between them. These songs also suggest two conflicting uses of art: the state's use of art to protect the status quo and the rebels' to protest it. Rather surprisingly, given the political tenor of the two zones, the songs of Zone Three are reactionary and those of Zone Four revolutionary in spirit. Zone Three, for example, is so intent on isolating itself from its barbaric neighbors it teaches its children that ''Great to Small/ High to Low/ Four into Three/ Cannot go'' (3). In contrast to these socially conservative lyrics, those sung by the women of Zone Four reverberate with social protest. Every three months, in fact, they celebrate song fests during which they violate the laws against cloud-gathering and keep alive the revolutionary spirit by trying to imagine what Zone Three is like. Although what they do is technically forbidden, those in power look the other way, giving tacit approval to these ritual protests. The changes wrought by the two political marriages are so pervasive that by the time the narrative ends, even the socially conservative Zone Three has been invaded by the revolutionary popular songs that have originated in Zone Five. For example, just before Al•Ith disappears into Zone Two, her friend Dabeeb brings her the following lyrics: "No, sting my self-contents to hunger/Till I ride my heart to the high lands/ Leaving myself behind" (228). This song specifically encourages people to visit other zones, a journey that will result in personal change because the travelers, like Al•Ith herself, will leave their old ways behind.

If the zones feel differently about intermingling, so too do they interpret common events differently.[13] When Al•Ith arrives in Zone Four for the first time, for example, she is not riding the horse that was sent for her use. As this information reaches the people, it stimulates two completely different reactions in the two zones. In Zone Four, because her behavior does not fit with their expectations of what a queen should do, the "riderless horse caused rumors to spread that Al•Ith had fallen and was dead" (26). Even after the people have learned that she is alive, a popular ballad still arises to the effect that the "willing bride is dead./ The realm she rules is cold and dark" (26). In contrast to this negative—and mendacious—interpretation, that of Zone Three is more positive. These people interpret the fact that Al•Ith is not on her horse as a sign of "loving friendship" (27). Zone Four's interpretation reflects the fact that they do not want this alien queen whom the Providers have sent them, and it shows their rather bleak outlook on life—an outlook born of their continual grinding poverty. Zone Three's interpretation reflects the emotional bond they feel with their queen and with their animals—a bond that until Al•Ith's arrival had been completely unknown to Zone Four.

Like these ballads, the graphic arts of the two zones also illustrate the tendency of a people to read a situation from their own experience and needs and to create art that meets these needs. In only a few instances do the visual accounts coincide with one another. Of the differences, the Chronicler says that there is always—"there has to be!—a difference between the way their artists and ours portray the various incidents in the tale of our queen and their king" (146). The scene that Lusik reports as being most popular with Zone Four, that of Al•Ith parading with Ben Ata before his armies while she is pregnant, was for a long time ignored in Zone Three's art because of its negative implications. Those who do paint the scene always focus on the fact that Al•Ith is subordinate to Ben Ata, some even showing her "with bound hands, or a chain around her neck" (148). Over time, however, the artists of both zones begin to represent this scene in much the same way, suggesting that the two zones themselves are beginning to change. In these revised representations, although the artists accurately portray Al•Ith's symbolic or official role, they still fail to express her "real feelings as she rode behind Ben Ata" (148). According to Lusik, the artists do not realize that while she might have been resentful of her lesser role in other circumstances, here she has accepted it as "necessary" (149). Observing Ben Ata in his role as "representative and leader of his men," therefore, she is able to admire and even love him for being "in command of what was needed from him" (148-49). Given her understanding of what is required from her in this situation, Lusik believes that the artists of Zone Four come closest to the truth when they picture "the child already born and some-times even on his own little horse riding in front of both Ben Ata and Al•Ith" (149). This view is more accurate because even Al•Ith recognizes the fact that she merely symbolizes the "channel or vessel" through which their new leader will be born (156).

Although Al•Ith is not recognized in her own right in Zone Four, she is nonetheless the novel's heroine. She is the heroine because it is largely due to her beneficent influence on her husband that he and his zone begin to change, just as it is due to her example that her own zone begins to change. But if Al•Ith is the novel's heroine, it is Lusik who is its triple "I": the informing consciousness that brings meaning to the marriage, the "eye" that leads his people from ignorance to understanding, and the "aye" that affirms that the actions of Al•Ith are necessary for the renewal of her land. His role as mediator to his people is critical because once Al•Ith leaves, they remember her only "with distaste" (142). As we have seen, when she returns to her own zone, after the lengthy sojourn in Zone Four, her people fail to recognize her as their queen; because of the changes she has undergone, they literally do not know who she is and eventually select her sister Murti• to replace her. According to Lusik, the accounts of Al•Ith's behavior that the people pass among themselves make "her sound bizarre . . . tainted and con-taminated" (142). One of his purposes in writing this chronicle, then, is to "revive in the hearts and memories of our people another idea of Al•Ith, to *re-state* her in her proper place in our history" (142-43; the emphasis is mine, but the pun is surely Lessing's). To educate his people he cannot use a direct approach, however, as he has discovered that it is only "through the unexpected . . . or the indirect that truths come our way" (140).[14] Rather than pushing his people to learn, as Al•Ith did in her abortive song fest, therefore, Lusik simply shows them—and us—"the sight of events in action" (141).

In its depiction of Lusik, this novel is perhaps more clearly expressive of Lessing's artistic philosophy than any of her previous fiction, for it shows both an artist's commitment to change and the effectiveness of individual action. As we have already seen, Lessing outlines her sense of artistic responsibility in "The Small Personal Voice" (see especially chapter 1 above). There, dismissing the image of the writer in an ivory tower as a dishonest one, she argues that the truly committed writer is one who functions "as an instrument of change for good or for bad".[15] Twenty-three years later, in *The Marriages Between Zones Three, Four, and Five*, she shows us just what she means by this artistic commitment. In the first place, Lusik acknowledges that he is an instrument of change. In fact, like Charles Watkins and the Survivor, he is on the front line of change, protected by nothing more than his own sense of purpose. Although he serves in an official capacity as chronicler, he does not enjoy the immortal status of Johor or the other Canopean emissaries. What he writes, therefore, is not informed by any kind of galactic intelligence or perspective. All interpretations are his own and limited to his personal capabilities as an artist. As he is well aware, it is this personal interpretation of public events that makes the role of the artist so crucial in a time of crisis. Not only does he create the world for us, his extra-textual readers, but he also creates it for his intra-textual readers. He does so by bringing shape and meaning to those events he witnesses and in so doing giving his people a new view of their world. He is, indeed, their guide-leader, leading them surely into another realm of experience.

Just as he stands for change, he also expresses Lessing's ideas that as a writer he should speak for those who cannot speak for themselves. As one of Al•Ith's Mind-Fathers (the men who nourish a child's spirit) and as the official chronicler of her activities, for example, Lusik writes that he shares "in Al•Ith's condition of being ruler insofar as I can write of her, describe her" (198). This statement seems to have many meanings. It means, on the one hand, that he participates in Al•Ith's activities by recording them. It also means that as Chronicler, as author, he rules his people because he defines reality for them. Beyond this, Lusik shares "in Al•Ith's condition of being ruler" because, as he puts it, we are "the visible and evident aspects of a whole we all share, that we all go to form" (197). When Lusik writes of Al•Ith, therefore, he becomes "woman with her" (198). If, as he suggests, we are all parts of a whole, the way in which particular individuals manifest themselves at any given time depends on "how these needs are pulled out of us" (197). During the time encompassed by this chronicle, what the people of Zone Three needed most was representation. This need was met by Al•Ith who represented their way of life to Zone Four and thus eased the tensions between the two countries, and it was further met by Lusik who represented to them the meaning of her marriage to Ben Ata. In other words, Al•Ith embodies and Lusik authors the new world created by her marriage to Zone Four. While Al•Ith, who is the "substance of Zone Three," explores new geographies of the mind and heart, her discoveries are recorded by Lusik, who gives them meaning and significance (197). Because of her own people's resistance to her change, without the efforts of Lusik the Chronicler, those of Al•Ith the Queen would have been for naught.

And, finally, Lusik reflects Lessing's description of a responsible artist by trying to strike a balance between the competing poles of a dialectic.[16] As we have already seen, although the novel does not fall into separate conflicting sections as do Lessing's earlier novels, the pattern here is still one of dialectics, as both Al•Ith and Ben Ata represent conflicting ways of life. And even though they constitute the novel's major dialectic, they are not its only example, as others are suggested between Al•Ith and Vahshi and between Zone Two and all the other zones. In describing these dialectics, Lusik seems to suggest that even evil can have a positive role in the process of change. It is a role he acknowledges but is loath to describe in any detail.[17] In the passage I have already cited where Lusik describes his identification as an artist with Al•Ith the Queen, he also warns of the dangers of such identification. Of the dangers he says that writers "do well to be afraid when we approach those parts of our histories (our natures) that deal with evil, the depraved, the benighted'' (198). The danger for him lies not only in becoming evil but in summoning it. Yet, even with these dangers ever present, he contends it is absolutely imperative that we recognize the necessity for such evils to exist. He writes that "without this sting of otherness, of—even—the vicious, without the terrible energies of the underside of health, sanity, sense, then nothing works or *can* work" (198; Lessing's emphasis).

What is remarkable is not so much that Lusik takes this position, but that, as a narrator of Lessing's, he is so unwilling to describe it in full. It is almost as though Lessing herself were afraid of the evil she herself might have loosed on the world by describing what is wrong with it. At the same time she is unwilling to portray evil, she is eager to portray its counterpart—in what may be the most optimistic book of her career. Certainly in its emphasis on what is good in life and what is possible for people to achieve in terms of changing themselves, this novel is unique in the Lessing canon. It is as though with it Lessing were offering us the utopia she only hinted at in Martha Quest's visions of the four-gated city and tantalizingly withdrew from us at the last moment in *The Memoirs of a Survivor*. Seen in this light, the novel seems to fulfill Lessing's own call to arms in "The Small Personal Voice," where she asked, "What is the choice before us? It is not merely a question of preventing an evil, but of strengthening a vision of a good which may defeat the evil" ("SPV," 190). It is perhaps out of this conviction that she has written this utopian fabulation, in which she can give us a vision of good to nourish our hope and our imagination.

At the same time she gives us hope, she also instructs us in how we too might change. She shows us, for example, how marriage changes Al•Ith, Ben Ata, and Vahshi for the better. She also shows us how the graphic, written, and oral art forms—taking these marriages as their subject matter—can lead to social change by helping people to expand their horizons and introducing them to the unknown. By using these examples, Lessing calls our attention to the need for change and invites us to change ourselves. Just as Lusik's chronicle has a salutary effect on his story audience, it should have a similar salutary effect on us. As we witness the changes that take place in Al•Ith and Ben Ata, we too are changed.

As we see them comparing their own incompatible worldviews, we too, as part of the reading process itself, make similar comparisons. When we see their discomfort in being faced with alien worldviews, we recognize our own discomfort. We do so because even as we read we are being confronted with the alien worldview of the novel itself. Just as they are challenged by the unknown, so we are. And as they rethink their position on various political and philosophical issues, we rethink ours—again simply by virtue of reading the text.[18] Through the combination of her story line and her narrative techniques, Lessing has given us a model for change. In Al•Ith and Ben Ata she is showing us how two people, who fully participate in society in a responsible fashion, can make fundamental changes in their own thinking and behavior simply by being open to different ideas. And in the way she tells her story, Lessing invites us to emulate the changes she describes.

As the chronicler authors the changes in his world through his narration, so he functions as the *author*ity we need in order to understand Lessing's purpose in writing this book. In effect, in this novel the guide-leader has become one with the artist. Like Lessing's other narrators, Lusik is guide-leader both to his story audience and to us. His purpose in addressing both audiences is to change his readers' perceptions by introducing a compelling reason to participate in his vision of cosmic unity. His success with his own people lies in his ability to convince them to share the perspective of the other zones. His success with us is determined by his ability to convince us of the need to enter new realms of experience. By book's end, if he has represented Lessing well, his narrative itself will have served for us as a visit to another zone, during which time we will have found a new way to see the world. The success he achieves internally and externally is a direct result of his skills in artistic mediation. In his efforts to transform his own world, he receives the help of its songmakers and artists. In his efforts to change us, he is limited to his own talents as a writer. Just as Al•Ith represents and embodies Zone Three, therefore, Lusik represents and embodies Lessing. Like her he stands between two worlds, translating the meaning of one into images and concepts that can be comprehended by the other. That is, he constitutes the voice of Lessing that is at the heart of this novel, guiding her readers through the mysterious zones of yet another unexpected universe, where even the dialectics of sex can be seen as necessary to the process of individual and social change.

NOTES

1. It is worth noting in this context how much Lessing herself likes this novel. In a recent interview with Minda Bikman, Lessing is quoted as saying, "There's never been a book that I enjoyed writing as much as that one. It was a piece of cake, very unlike most of my books, which are agony. I really loved it" ("A Talk with Doris Lessing," *New York Times Book Review*, 30 March 1980, p. 24).

2. According to Lesley Hazleton, Lessing herself "stresses that they should be read independently" ("Doris Lessing on Feminism, Communism and 'Space Fiction,' " *New York Times Magazine*, 25 July 1982, p. 21).

3. For a discussion of the novel's symbolism, see Roberta Rubenstein, "*The Marriages Between Zones Three, Four, and Five*: Doris Lessing's Alchemical Allegory," *Science Fiction Studies*, 24, no. 3 (Fall 1983), 201-15. Finding it "a condensed and highly allegorical narrative," Rubenstein suggests that it takes its symbolism from the "alchemical marriage, in which the sacred union represents an aspect of the 'work' toward the ultimate goal of inner enlightenment" (201, 203).

4. Doris Lessing, *The Marriages Between Zones Three, Four, and Five (as narrated by the Chroniclers of Zone Three)* (New York: Alfred A. Knopf, 1980), 4. Subsequent page references appear in the text.

5. There is some disagreement among critics as to the significance of the characters' names in this novel. See, for example, Rochelle Cleary, "What's in a Name? Lessing's Message in *The Marriages Between Zones Three, Four, and Five,*" *Doris Lessing Newsletter*, 6, no. 2 (Winter 1982), 8-10; and Claire Sprague's rebuttal, "Naming in *Marriages*: Another View," *Doris Lessing Newsletter*, 7, no. 1 (Summer 1983), 13.

6. What sets this institution apart from the others, besides its positive portrait here, is the fact that it is divided into units small enough for the members to know one another as individuals and thus help to keep its "rules" and "regulations" flexible. For a comprehensive look at Lessing's treatment of marriage, see Rochelle Cleary, "A Study of Marriage in Doris Lessing's Fiction," *DAI*, 42 (1981), 4831A (State University of New York at Stony Brook).

7. Shulamith Firestone, *The Dialectic of Sex: The Case for Feminist Revolution* (1970; rpt. New York: Bantam Books, 1971).

8. Herbert Marcuse, *An Essay on Liberation* (Boston: Beacon Press, 1969). Here he imagines a situation where the "liberated consciousness would promote the development of a science and technology free to discover and realize the possibilities of things and men in the protection and gratification of life, playing with the potentialities of form and matter for the attainment of this goal" (24). For more on Marcuse, see the introduction above.

9. For another discussion of the various oppositions in the novel, see Marsha Rowe, " 'If you mate a swan and a gander, who will ride?' " in *Notebooks/ Memoirs/ Archives: Reading and Rereading Doris Lessing*, ed. Jenny Taylor (Boston and London: Routledge & Kegan Paul, 1982), 191-205.

10. In "Communicating Differently: Doris Lessing's *Marriages Between Zones Three, Four, and Five*," Ellen Peel discusses this point by addressing the question of communication among the zones (*Doris Lessing Newsletter*, 6, no 2 [Winter 1982], 11-13). Treating the novel as a "fable of communication" (11), Peel describes how the "Female, egalitarian Zone Three" and the "male, hierarchical Zone Four" (12) learn to overcome the different kinds of discourse that initially separate them, concluding that in this novel "Communication causes, results from, and symbolizes the appreciation of difference" (13).

11. The same image of embodiment appears on page 256 of *The Sirian Experiments* when Ambien II describes the ruling coalition on Sirius as the Five who "embody the governance of our Empire. That is what we *are*" (New York: Alfred A. Knopf, 1980; Lessing's emphasis).

12. Michael Polanyi, *The Tacit Dimension* (1966; rpt. Garden City, N.Y.: Anchor Books, 1967), 15. On this subject, see also *Knowing and Being: Essays by Michael Polanyi*, ed. Marjorie Grene (1969; rpt. Chicago: University of Chicago Press, 1974), especially part 3, "Tacit Knowing," where he says that "To use language in speech, reading and writing, is to extend our bodily equipment and become intelligent human beings. We may say that when we learn to use language, or a probe, or a tool, and thus make ourselves aware of these things as we are of our body, we *interiorize* these things and *make ourselves dwell in them*. Such extensions of ourselves develop new faculties in us; our whole education operates in this way; as each of us interiorizes our cultural heritage, he grows into a person seeing the world and experiencing life in terms of this outlook" (148; Polanyi's emphases). This is similar to the point I make about language and perception in chapter 7 below. Lessing also alludes to bodily knowledge in *Shikasta* when Johor reports that David and Sais "*could* not believe in death for themselves" because those "robust bodies knew that hundreds of years of life lay ahead, and their bodies' knowledge

was stronger than the feeble thoughts of their impaired minds" (*Shikasta* [New York: Alfred A. Knopf, 1979], 71; Lessing's emphasis).

13. In her essay on this novel, Roberta Rubenstein focuses on the symbolism of these references to artistic representation, references that she finds "suggest the variations and mythical heightenings that are analogous to the layers of meaning hidden in alchemical texts, and the equal possibility of misunderstanding or misreading those texts" ("Allegory," 204).

14. Although Lessing is clearly a didactic novelist, she is not unaware of the power of indirection as is suggested by her debts to Sufi literature. On this subject, see two essays by Nancy Shields Hardin: "Doris Lessing and the Sufi Way," *Contemporary Literature*, 14, no. 4 (Autumn 1973), 565-81; and "The Sufi Teaching Story and Doris Lessing," *Twentieth Century Literature*, 23, no. 3 (October 1977), 314-25.

15. Doris Lessing, "The Small Personal Voice," in *Declaration*, ed. by Tom Maschler (c. 1957; New York: E. P. Dutton & Co., 1958), 190. A subsequent page reference appears in the text as "SPV."

16. According to Roberta Rubenstein, in this novel Lessing "feels she successfully achieves the anonymous, timeless voice of the storyteller who observes without judging" ("An Evening at the 92nd Street Y," *Doris Lessing Newsletter*, 8, no. 2 [Fall 1984], 6).

17. Lessing has another passage on this subject in *The Sentimental Agents*, where Ambien describes Tafta's occupation as popular writer and apologist for technology. Of his fiction, Ambien remarks, "This type of fiction was both challenging and useful, in that it gave the populace opportunities to examine potentialities of technological discoveries: but also anodyne, because the mere fact that sometimes appalling developments had been displayed in print at all seemed to reassure the citizens that they could not happen" ([New York: Alfred A. Knopf, 1981], 279). This reminds me of the passage in Charles Child Walcutt's *American Literary Naturalism: A Divided Stream*, where he accuses science fiction writers of "domesticating" and "promoting the very horror they set out to expose" ([Minneapolis: University of Minnesota Press, 1956], 14).

18. As Ellen Peel puts it so well, "No matter how much readers resist the book's persuasion toward otherness, they surrender simply by reading, for the very process introduces the thought of the other into the self" ("Communicating Differently," 11).

5.

Visions and Revisions: *The Sirian Experiments*

In *The Sirian Experiments* (1981), Lessing leaves the fabulous Zones of Three, Four, and Five and returns again to Shikasta, using the same kinds of political commentary and defamiliarization that marked the first novel in her series. But even with these similarities, there are important differences between the two books, especially as regards their narrators. Johor's acknowledged purpose in writing, it will be recalled, is primarily to convince his fellow Canopeans to continue their policy of intervening in the politics of Shikasta; at the same time, he unknowingly functions outside the text as an advocate of Lessing's philosophy of wholeness. In making his case, of course, he affirms the basic principles of his empire. On the other hand, Ambien II, one of the five co-equal rulers of Sirius, abandons the principles of her empire for those of Canopus—its archenemy. As a recent convert, she has voluntarily assumed the task of trying to persuade her fellow Sirian rulers that they too should follow the Canopean way. In short, she is recommending a complete reversal of official government policy. Her text is therefore much more politically explosive than Johor's—and her actions more courageous as she takes a stand that she knows will mean her downfall as one of the five rulers of Sirius. Although much of what she does distinguishes her from Johor, like him she too functions as Lessing's advocate, indirectly addressing us on the merits of Canopean philosophy even as she tries to get her fellow rulers to reform.

In documenting her conversion, Ambien shows no inclination to engineer a coup that would overthrow the other rulers in power at the time. Her express purpose is to change their perspective—not unseat them. Given the fact that she is not seeking personal power, it is surely significant that she would question the very foundation of Sirian government, as she herself apparently has nothing to gain from this heretical behavior. Regardless of her altruistic motives, her defection from official policy leads to "planet arrest" on Colonised Planet 13, where she is expected to recognize the error of her ways and recant her position.[1] Like modern Soviet dissidents who are incarcerated under trumped up charges of insanity, Ambien is accused of having "succumbed to a mental disequilibrium, due to an overprolonged immersion in the affairs of the planet Rohanda" (287). This accusation appears in a "Directive from the Four," which identifies her narrative as being "the work of unfortunates who wish to subvert the good government of our Empire" (287). Ironically, rather than causing us to doubt Ambien ourselves, this statement has the opposite effect of increasing her credibility with us. This occurs because we have no reason at all to trust the other Sirian rulers and every reason to trust Ambien herself.[2]

Ambien has earned our trust because she shares our doubts about the superiority of Canopus and the Canopeans. Unconvinced that she really wants to become a Canopean, she expresses all the skepticism that has been building in us throughout the series, as we too are resentful of a philosophy and point of view that make us look bad. By openly admitting her reservations about Canopus she disarms our doubts and helps to win us over to Lessing's position—much as the Survivor does by her candid admissions of disbelief.[3] By maintaining her skepticism throughout most of her narrative, Ambien seems truly to speak for us. Perhaps alone among Lessing's narrators, therefore, Ambien represents both the concerns of Lessing herself and those of Lessing's readers. In her advocacy of Canopean ideals she clearly represents Lessing. But in her initial reluctance to accept them, she also appears to represent us, Lessing's all-too-skeptical readers. Because she represents our feelings so well, once she accepts Canopean values as her own, she makes a very persuasive advocate for Lessing.

That Ambien is able to convince us, however imperfectly, of the rightness of her cause can be explained not only by the fact that she is a former skeptic with whom we can identify but also by the fact that she is the third narrator of the series. That is, in repeatedly representing the Canopean perspective, the series itself inevitably has a cumulative effect on us—even as we try to resist it. This effect builds to such a point that eventually we conspire in our own conversion. For example, in the fifth book a Canopean agent says of Sirius that they have just begun to understand that "an Empire may control its development according to . . . but that is another story."[4] The ellipsis is Lessing's, but we have been programmed so successfully by the preceding four novels that it is impossible for us not to plug in the word "necessity" when we come to the blank. We may not believe the slogan "according to necessity"—or even fully understand it—but we certainly know it by heart because we have heard it so often. This may sound like a narrative gimmick on Lessing's part, but I do not discount its importance even as a gimmick as we have only to turn on our televisions to experience what Kenneth Burke has identified as the "power of endless repetition."[5]

The technique of endless repetition is not only used by advertisers to make us memorize the name of a product; it can also be used with more dire consequences. Burke describes, for example, how Hitler used it in conjunction with other psychological strategies to foment the anti-Jewish sentiments that led to the Holocaust. In another context, Herbert Marcuse refers to a similar process of wearing down people's resistance that can be achieved through the use of what he calls "hypnotic formulas."[6] According to Marcuse, the "fact that a specific noun is almost always coupled with the same 'explicatory' adjectives and attributes makes the sentence into a *hypnotic formula* which, *endlessly repeated*, fixes the meaning in the recipient's mind" (91; my emphases). Although "according to necessity" is not the kind of grammatical construction that Marcuse identifies as being particularly pernicious, the principle he describes still holds true. Throughout Lessing's series, whenever anything occurs that is particularly difficult to comprehend, vis-à-vis the reasons something must be done or even how it must be done, the explanation offered by the Canopeans is inevitably the catch phrase "according to necessity." This is a vague response, almost totally incomprehensible to Western minds. Through the simple but unrelenting process of repetition, however, it assumes the force of truth and the appearance of a real explanation. (For more on this, see the discussion in chapter 7 on debunking.)

The phrase is something with which Ambien certainly has a great deal of trouble, trouble that we share, as most of us are skeptical of vague abstractions that are posited as solutions to complex political problems. But skeptic though she begins, Ambien II eventually does accept the principle of "according to necessity." And, although we may retain a healthy skepticism even after finishing *The Sirian Experiments*, we too have been subjected to the power of endless repetition until we do tend to believe with her that the Canopeans may have something to teach us after all. The reason we come to roughly the same conclusion is that we all have benefited from the instruction of guide-leaders. Ambien's guide-leaders are Klorathy, a Canopean agent who tutors her, and Nasar/Rhodia, a Canopean agent whom she observes in two different human guises. Our guide-leaders, of course, have been Johor and Lusik, both of whom have, in one way or another, prepared us to receive the additional guidance of Ambien herself. Whatever the differences among these three narrators, the messages they convey are all mutually supportive of one another. Thus it is that, although Ambien might be a voice crying in the wilderness among her own people, she is part of a larger voice outside the text, that voice being composed of the other narrators of Lessing's science fiction.

Because she is not the first of Lessing's narrators to introduce us to the ideas behind *Canopus in Argos*, her responsibility as guide-leader is slightly different from that of the others. Like the other narrators, Ambien translates the details of an alien frame of reference and philosophy into something we can understand—having an easier job of it perhaps because she is the third narrator of the series. But at the same time, she faces the more difficult task of trying to make this alien world come alive in this particular novel without tediously repeating what we already know from the earlier ones. This is not meant to imply that she should avoid the formulaic repetition that helps to build Lessing's case. It is meant to suggest the kind of narrative pitfalls facing the author of a polemical and non-linear series like *Canopus in Argos*, where, for the sake of argument and clarity, the temptation always is to rehash the same ideas from novel to novel. To rehash them, of course, risks losing the reader who does not want to hear the same things over and over again. But if the novel—especially a science fiction novel—is to stand on its own, it must repeat at the very least the premises of the earlier works. In solving this narrative problem, Lessing has devised several strategies that together satisfactorily maintain reader interest, forward the story line, and reinforce the same ideas she has introduced us to earlier.

One way she keeps our interest is through the previously mentioned device of using a skeptical narrator. Another way is by using her own fictional Line of Demarcation that like its fifteenth-century predecessor divides the world into two spheres of influence and thus provides the reader with two different sets of data. What we have taking place in *The Sirian Experiments*, therefore, is both extra-textual and inter-textual recognition, as we recognize in an alien context information that turns our attention to events in history and events in *Shikasta*. The result is that, like Ambien II herself, we find ourselves questioning virtually everything we encounter as we try to fit together a meaningful pattern composed of three often conflicting perspectives: Sirian, Canopean, and our own. Thus the same narrator who translates the details of two alien frames of reference into something we can understand conversely functions to defamiliarize both empirical and textual reality for us. This is what makes reading *The Sirian Experiments* epistemologically unsettling, as we are continually having to redefine our view of the world as we recognize ourselves in both the Sirian and the Canopean frames.[7]

The Line of Demarcation that Lessing uses does not divide the world longitudinally between the Spanish and the Portuguese, but latitudinally between the Canopeans and the Sirians. We learn in *Shikasta* that the Canopeans are given the northern hemisphere to develop and the Sirians the southern hemisphere. Therefore, most of what Johor defamiliarizes for us has to do with the history of Europe and North America (especially the United States). And most of what Ambien II defamiliarizes has to do with Africa and South America. We are reminded of the cargo cults of Africa, for example, when Ambien describes a tribe of Lombis singing about "shining machines" and raising their faces "in supplication to the skies" (34). Another tribe she describes, located apparently somewhere in Central America called Grakconkranpatl, ritually murders its sacrificial victims by cutting their hearts out while they are still alive; this practice seems to defamiliarize the rituals held in honor of the principle Aztec deity—Quetzalcoatl (166). Ambien also describes in detail the disappearance of an island paradise called Adalantaland, which is no doubt a reference to the lost continent of Atlantis (82). At one point she encounters Ghenjis Khan who is named here "Ghonkez"—but he is also described as being part of the "Mongol" [sic] threat (253). Because all the other historical references throughout the novel have been disguised, we are startled to encounter a reference in its original form—just as we were startled to see the phrase "World War II" in *Shikasta*. Our reaction in both instances suggests that we have on some level accepted the defamiliarized version of history that Lessing invents in her texts.

In addition to this extra-textual historical recognition, there are also many examples of inter-textual recognition, where Ambien refers to things we already know from reading *Shikasta*. One example, which is discussed more fully below, is that of the Conference between Canopus and Sirius, during which Rohanda was evenly divided between the two empires. Another example is the reference to the "degenerative disease," a concept we understand even if Ambien doesn't explain it here (43). There are also several passages that deal with how Sirius has meddled with human evolution; these passages, while different from their counterparts in *Shikasta*, do serve as a kind of inter-textual recognition as we inevitably compare the brutal Sirian interference with the benign Canopean guidance. One notable example of inter-textual recognition (which I mentioned above in chapter 3), is a complete passage that appears verbatim in both novels. This is the "Private letter sent through the Diplomatic Bag" from Ambien II to Klorathy, in which she describes the mental deterioration of the Shammatan agents during the Century of Destruction (*Shikasta*, 265; *The Sirian Experiments*, 284). As I suggested earlier, these repeated passages help to reinforce both Lessing's cosmology and the basic philosophical premises of the series. They also serve as literary allusions, enriching the text in which they appear by referring to similar passages in an earlier novel. But, ultimately, in conjunction with the previously cited examples of external recognition, they help to make us self-conscious readers.

The purpose of all this recognition and our attendant self-consciousness, as it has been in the previous novels, is to get us to change our frame of reference. Like *The Memoirs of a Survivor*,

The Sirian Experiments provides us with two alternatives from which to choose. Instead of two different worlds, however, here we are given two different worldviews—Canopean and Sirian. The differences between the two philosophies are primarily moral ones that leave Sirius feeling defensive about its policies. Ambien herself is only too aware of her empire's defensiveness, noting that her work is "an attempt at a re-interpretation of history, from a certain point of view. An unpopular point of view, even now: until recently, impossible" (8). This point of view would have been impossible because Sirians are apparently immune to the truth, especially when it involves Canopus—an empire that is morally, technologically, and militarily superior to Sirius. Although all available evidence points in this direction, Sirius refuses to acknowledge the fact, preferring to think of Canopus as morally unfit and technologically inept. To protect the myth of its own superiority, therefore, the Sirian rulers, like so many totalitarian governments that have been threatened by the truth, are not above bending it to suit themselves. Although Sirius lost the war with Canopus, for example, its leaders advertise this defeat as a "truce" so they "would not suffer ignomy in the eyes of [their] fellow states and empires" (9). Like the propagandizing efforts of the state in Orwell's *1984*, those of the Sirian rulers extend to doctoring historical records, from which they remove "any hint" that they had lost the war with Canopus (9). The Sirians are so insistent on seeing Canopus as an enemy, in fact, that they fail to see that Canopus in reality is trying to help them. Whenever Canopus has given them information, therefore, the Sirians have automatically considered it to be false and misleading. In short, the Sirian "set of mind has been one that has *consistently* led [them] into wrong judgement" (9; Lessing's emphasis).

Ambien indicates the bad judgment shown by her empire in her description of the conference held between Canopus and Sirius on Colony 10, during which they divided Rohanda between themselves and laid out plans for the future of the planet. In her description of this conference, Ambien repeats several details that we remember from *Shikasta*, thus providing us with many examples of inter-textual recognition. Among the things she describes are the Lock between Canopus and Rohanda, the importation of the giants from Colony 10, and the eventual symbiosis between them and the planet's indigenous inhabitants. Because we already know all this, there is an ironic distance between us and Ambien at this point. We have seen the good that Canopus does on Shikasta. But the Sirians, including Ambien herself at this point, are suspicious of its motives, assuming that Canopus is as untrustworthy as they are. In part this comes from the fact that they use words differently, with Canopus using them as much as possible to reflect reality and Sirius to disguise it. For example, when Sirius uses words such as "harmony, good fellowship, co-operation"—which are the same words that Canopus uses to describe its relationship to Rohanda—they "do not mean by them what Canopus means" (10). Other misunderstandings arise because the Sirians won't take at face value the information that Canopus freely gives them. Sirius is suspicious because they are "handicapped by being resentful" of their competitor (11). They are resentful because they have convinced themselves that Canopus, in taking the northern hemisphere to colonize, is " 'as usual' grabbing the best of everything," leaving Sirius the lesser part (11). What they have conveniently forgotten is that they have no sovereign right to any part of the planet which had been discovered by Canopus in the first place.

As a Sirian, Ambien II is not always immune to bad judgment herself—especially when it comes to misusing the language, a weakness Klorathy is always trying to correct in her. After Canopus has renamed the planet Shikasta, for example, she stubbornly insists on calling it Rohanda, even though the name is no longer accurate. Remarking on the possible consequences of this Sirian habit, Klorathy warns her that "if one did not use the exact and correct words then one's thinking would soon become unclear and confused" (90). He offers similar advice when the earth's magnetic poles reverse and Adalantaland is swept under water. Ambien is horrified and calls what happens a "catastrophe" (89). Klorathy views it differently and in an annoyingly pedantic exchange tells her that a "Catastrophe, or, to use the absolutely accurate and correct word, Disaster . . . , could only properly be applied to a *real* misfortune, a true evolutionary setback, namely, the failure of the Lock" (89; Lessing's emphasis). According to him, because the reversal of the poles and the disappearance of Adalantaland did not "in any fundamental way alter the nature of Rohanda," it would be more accurate to describe what happened as "events"—this even though the entire planet had been wracked by climatic changes, earthquakes, and other physical upheavals (90). Because Klorathy is so utterly precise in his choice of words, these lessons suggest that Canopus understands the relationship between the language we use and the reality we see. But regardless of his admirable precision, our sympathies lie with Ambien, who, in her nostalgic references to Rohanda and her horror at the destruction of Adalantaland, comes much closer to describing our attitudes than does the cosmically minded Klorathy. If these are examples of her bad judgment, as they are certainly presented, we can only identify with them, an identification that helps further to cement our trust in Ambien herself.

It is out of the desire to correct the self-destructive attitudes of her people that Ambien has determined to set the record straight. She does this out of her conviction that "the duty of a historian is to tell the truth as far as possible" (5). What amazes her the most as she retraces her own changes is that the truth had always been available to the Sirians. For example, instead of sending spies into the northern hemisphere to check on the activity of the Canopeans, "All we needed," Ambien writes, "was to read, without suspicion and with an open mind, the material they continually supplied us and then to ask them questions" (46). In looking back at her own behavior, she confesses that she has to "marvel" at her former "blindness"—a blindness that characterizes all Sirians (59).

The inability of her people to look at themselves with a "dispassionate, disinterested eye" arises from the fact that they have been historically "preoccupied by one basic *physical* fact and the questions caused thereby since its inception: technology: our technical achievements that no other empire has ever even approached" (61-62; Lessing's emphasis). The Sirians' conviction that they are superior arises primarily out of their definition of technology. "The subtle, infinitely varied, hard-to-see technology of Canopus," Ambien points out, "was invisible to us, and therefore for all these millennia, these long ages, we have counted ourselves as supreme" (62). To her amazement, even at the close of their Dark Age, the Sirians *"still did not know how to look at"* themselves (63; Lessing's emphasis). Because of this willful blindness, whenever they consult with Canopus, they are unable to benefit from the exchange. In its emphasis on Sirian arrogance, this passage cannot help but call to mind the Western arrogance of mind that historically has prevented us from even recognizing, let alone respecting, the technology of so-called primitive tribes.

Because of her own change of perspective regarding Canopus, Ambien is only too aware of the fact that all of us "see truths when we can see them" (8). Behind her desire to set the record straight, therefore, is the other desire to show her readers the process by which she came to see the truth. What this process involves more than anything is learning to ask the right questions. Until she learns what to ask, the answers she gets from Klorathy, instead of informing simply infuriate her—as they infuriate us. For example, when she and he discuss the differences between the cities on Canopus and those on Rohanda, she wants to know why they are shaped differently. When he tells her that they "are designed according to need," she thinks to herself: "*Well, obviously*" (68; Lessing's emphasis). In another passage, she describes an exchange Ambien I has with Klorathy, in which Klorathy admits that he plans to stay with a group of savages "*until they asked the right questions*" (91; Lessing's emphasis). When Ambien I further asks why Klorathy even expects them to be able to ask the "necessary questions in their own good time," he replies, "Because I am here" (91). Ambien II, hearing of this, feels "irritated to the point of fury" (91). Later when she and Klorathy meet again on Planet 11, which is inhabited by Colony 10 Giants and intelligent insects, Ambien is so repulsed by the insects that she asks Klorathy why he spends so much time among them. He replies, "At this time, for our present needs, this planet is important to us" (104). Even though she recognizes that "this reply was specific, and contained information" she has wanted, she is still unable to overcome her aversion to the insect creatures and longs for nothing more than to leave the planet (104).

Before she leaves, however, she asks what she realizes is a "real question: one that he had been waiting for me to ask" (105). To his statement that the giants and the insects "are a balance for each other. Together they make a whole," she has countered with: "*In relation to what?*" (105; Lessing's emphasis). Although she knows she has asked the right question, she is still not advanced enough in her thinking to accept the answer he gives her in reply. When he (predictably) tells her, "In relation to *need*," she snaps back, "Need, need, need. You always say need. What need?" (105; Lessing's emphasis). To this outburst—which surely represents our own frustration—she gets no reply, as it is not a necessary question. Although most of their exchanges end in Ambien's becoming put out with what she sees as Klorathy's lack of cooperation, she is astute enough to recognize that if she could but "understand him and his ways" she would "understand . . . well, but that was after all the point!" (113; Lessing's ellipsis).

Perhaps the best expression of the process of change she is undergoing occurs midway through her account when she admits finally that what she is learning about Canopus is a "challenge to everything I was *as a Sirian official*" (156; Lessing's emphasis). There are two important points being made in this statement. One has to do with the fact that Ambien sees herself "first and foremost" as a Sirian (67). Or, as she says of Klorathy's purpose in instructing her, it was not "an individual matter. No, it was Canopus and Sirius—as always" (215). In other words, in her capacity as student, she is part and parcel of an all-powerful group mind known as the Sirian Empire. The other point has to do with the fundamental challenge to her very being that the Canopean position represents. Torn between her loyalty to Sirius and her growing conviction that Canopus is "altogether finer and higher" than Sirius, she admits that, as a trained observer, she simply has to "recognise facts" when she sees them (157). "*Facts*," she goes on to say, "the more experienced one became, were always to be understood, garnered, taken in, with that part of oneself most deeply involved with *processes*, with life as it worked its way out. Facts were *not* best as understood formulas or summings up, but through this inward groping and *recognition*" (157-58; Lessing's emphases).[8] What she begins to recognize is that her dealings with Canopus are intended to bring her "to a new view of the Sirian usage of the planet, a new view of ourselves altogether" (215). Although it pains her to admit that even she is subject to the Canopean necessity, she reports that, given the facts, she simply "could not dismiss it" (158). She is unable to do so because of the "steady, unstoppable growth" in her of an entity that is no longer " 'Sirius' " (158).

This is the same process of change, I would argue, that Lessing hopes her readers will engage in as we too confront the "finer and higher" Canopean philosophy of wholeness and necessity. Just as Ambien is confronted with the dialectics of change in having to choose between Sirian and Canopean ways, we too are confronted, not just with this conflict but with an additional one between our own frame of reference and those of the text. In her efforts to help us change, Ambien, like Lessing's other narrators, functions as our guide-leader. But she also functions as something of an internal devil's advocate—expressing the same doubts we ourselves have had in reading about Canopus. In so doing, she opens the text: representing two sides of the question even as she gradually replaces one frame of reference with another—a process not unlike what happens in *Shikasta* where Johor establishes the dominant frame of reference and Rachel Sherban and Chen Liu function as titular devil's advocates, representing the human point of view. The difference between these advocates and Ambien is that she is working from Sirian truths that we do not share. When she acknowledges the fact that we all see truths when we can, therefore, the principle applies to us only in general terms. It does not apply to this specific case because we are not ourselves Sirian. One example of where our truths deviate from hers takes place when she fails to see the good that Canopus does on Shikasta. She is unable to see the truth because she takes it as a given that all empires are as corrupt as hers. Although we can see, from our prior knowledge, that Canopus does indeed do good on Shikasta, we have trouble with Ambien's basic premises that these two great empires have influenced human evolution. As our guide-leader, therefore, Ambien is able to express our doubts, our nostalgia, and often our frustration, but she does not express our view of reality.

Even though this is true, she does approach our revised view of reality when she speaks as a Canopean convert. This development, which at the very least is unexpected, takes place for at least three reasons. One has to do with the fact that in *Shikasta* Johor has already established the frame of reference for the series, and it is a Canopean one. As we read the rest of the series, therefore, although we may not literally believe what we read, we do tend to accept the dominant view of reality that has been presented at the onset. When Ambien talks about the Sirian blindness that led to incorrect conclusions about Canopus, we agree almost automatically that Sirius has been wrong (9, 46, 59). We do so in part because we have no reason to think otherwise, which leads us to the second reason: the Sirian point of view has not been established previously and therefore we have no loyalty to it. Nor is it presented sympathetically in *The Sirian Experiments*. Although it is indeed thoroughly described, it is described from the perspective of someone who has pretty well dismissed it as self-serving and inferior. Because of this unflattering portrait of Sirius, when we see this empire in conflict with Canopus, we tend to reject its principles just as Ambien does. For example, Ambien tells us that she used to believe that if the Sirian "uses of Rohanda could not be described as having led to an improvement of the place, then the same had to be said about Canopus" (211). We know from her report that what she refers to is the fact that Sirius has used the planet to try to breed a slave population. These experiments Ambien has described in considerable detail—details that lead us to the inevitable comparison between the treatment of black slaves by whites and the medical experiments conducted on Jews by the Nazis. Nothing we learn in either novel suggests that Canopus has done anything even remotely as despicable as this. Knowing its innocence in these matters, we reject Ambien's assertions and thus help to affirm the metaphor of the entire series—that the Canopean worldview is superior to the Sirian's.

In short, we prefer Canopus over Sirius because, for the most part, we dislike the Sirian way of doing things. Although there are several places where I have shown that Ambien's attitudes reflect ours, the overall behavior of the Sirian Empire is not something with which we would want to identify or align ourselves. This is the third reason Canopus invites our loyalty: Lessing has stacked the deck against Sirius itself by portraying it in less than appealing terms. It may make us uncomfortable to learn that two extraterrestrial empires have influenced the course of human history, but given the choice between siding with Canopus or Sirius, we choose the lesser of two evils. In making this choice, we are ceding a bit of our own reality. In trying, like Ambien herself, to decide whether we prefer the Canopean or the Sirian way of doing things, we are engaged in a dialectic within the dialectic. We are having to choose between two conflicting views of life that both conflict with our own view. I am not trying to argue here that we ever entirely forego or forget our own reality base (that, of course, is a technical impossibility even in fiction). But I am arguing that in subjecting ourselves to the same conflict faced by Ambien, we do become immersed enough in this alien reality that we temporarily lose sight of our own. It is the same process that takes place in *The Memoirs of a Survivor*, where Lessing tries not to convince us of the literal existence of the world behind the wall but only to loosen our grasp on a dualistic view of reality.

Thus we begin to see the purpose of using a former Sirian representative as our guide-leader in this novel. As she conceived her series, Lessing no doubt was well aware that its ideas would meet with stubborn resistance among many of her readers. In this novel she is acknowledging our doubts and trying to lay them to rest. There is no place else in the series that our point of view as skeptical readers is better expressed than in Ambien II's angry response to Klorathy's pontificating. But as angry as she is at first, eventually she changes her mind about this Canopean pedantry and preaching. Like evangelists who use the testimony of recent converts, Lessing documents Ambien's reluctant conversion in the hope that it will be an inspiration for us to change too. Lessing has said of her narrator, "I could like Ambien II better than I do" (Preface, ix). I would suggest that Lessing does not like her as much as she could because Ambien represents the kind of chauvinistic pig-headedness Lessing is trying to correct in her readers. I am not even sure that Lessing's reservations about her character interfere with our response to her. I, for one, quite like her. And I certainly warm up to her when she gets mad at Klorathy. Lessing may feel a bit guilty about how she has done her character an injustice, but I think the sacrifice is effective. Somehow, Ambien II does manage to speak both for Lessing and for us. It is this balance that makes the novel worth reading. It is this balance that helps to win us over just a bit more to Lessing's Canopean ways. In recognizing our world in Rohanda and ourselves in Ambien, we continue to recognize who we are and what we do. Just as her encounters with Klorathy and Nasar/Rhodia lead Ambien to revise her worldview, our identification with her helps us to share her visions and revisions.

NOTES

1. Doris Lessing, *The Sirian Experiments: The Report by Ambien II, of the Five* (New York: Alfred A. Knopf, 1981), 286. Subsequent page references appear in the text. A note on names: although the narrator's full name is Ambien II, I often refer to her simply as Ambien. She is not to be confused with Ambien I, however, who is another (very minor) character.

2. This is a classic case of using an unreliable source to naturalize a text, to make it seem believable. For a discussion of the concept of naturalization see chapter 7, "Convention and Naturalization," in Jonathan Culler's *Structuralist Poetics: Structuralism, Linguistics, and the Study of Literature* (1975; rpt. New York: Cornell University Press, 1982), 131-60 (also discussed above in chapter 2).

3. On this narrative strategy, whereby a disarmingly candid narrator is used to naturalize something alien, see Jonathan Culler, *Structuralist Poetics* (pp. 149ff) cited above.

4. Doris Lessing, *Documents Relating to the Sentimental Agents in the Volyen Empire* (New York: Alfred A. Knopf, 1983), 21.

5. Kenneth Burke, "The Rhetoric of Hitler's 'Battle,' " in *The Philosophy of Literary Form: Studies in Symbolic Action*, 3d ed. (1941, 1967; rpt. Berkeley: University of California Press, 1973), 217.

6. Herbert Marcuse, *One-Dimensional Man: Studies in the Ideology of Advanced Industrial Society* (1964; rpt. Boston: Beacon Press, 1966), 91. Subsequent page references appear in the text.

7. This happens later, as I discuss below, in the next two novels where we are invited to recognize ourselves not just in Shikasta but in several more planets—all at the same time.

8. The question must arise here of whether or not the first clause of this sentence contains a typographical error. Given the structure of the second clause, it is reasonable to think that Lessing meant the sentence to read: "Facts were *not best understood as* formulas or summings up, but through this inward groping and recognition."

6.

Necessity and the New Physics:
The Making of the
Representative for Planet 8

As she has done throughout her series, in *The Making of the Representative for Planet 8* (1982) Lessing describes once again the ramifications of the Canopean concept of "necessity."[1] But the metaphor she has chosen to express her ideas here is strikingly different from those of the previous four novels. Here, for the first time, she takes her images and arguments directly from the field of modern physics—finally acknowledging the scientific principles that have informed all her science fiction. Although the principles of particle physics underlie Lessing's own philosophy of wholeness, her use of them in this novel is quite unexpected, given her previous negative portraits of the scientific community. In her earlier novels, it will be recalled, she portrayed science and its technological handmaiden primarily as bureaucratic monsters to be condemned for their abuses of nature and unchecked political power. But in *The Making of the Representative for Planet 8* she has recast science and technology as possible agents of human evolution and salvation. In assigning science and technology these unexpectedly positive roles, Lessing has acknowledged, if only implicitly, that scientific thought lends itself to more than technological-industrial applications; she has also implied that technology lends itself to something infinitely more subtle and liberating than merely a utilitarian transformation of our material environment—an idea she first alluded to in *The Sirian*

Experiments. Lessing's own change of heart regarding the role of science in modern life seems to stem from her understanding of particle physics.[2] As described by such eminent theoretical physicists as Werner Heisenberg and David Bohm, one of the important by-products of quantum mechanics has been the discovery that the universe is an undivided whole, full of unexpected relationships and paradoxical events—a perspective congruent with Lessing's own philosophy of life.

Lest it be thought that in its own unexpectedly positive attitude toward science this novel is only full of surprises for Lessing's readers, I should add here that a great deal of the novel is familiar to us from her earlier work. In fact, as I shall argue, there is much in the book to suggest that it is the thematic and dramatic conclusion to *Canopus in Argos.* Because of its apparent thematic fulfillment of the first three novels of the series, it is not surprising that there is also a rhetorical similarity among them in their common use of recognition, re-cognition, and a narrative guide-leader. In short, like the other novels in the series, *Planet 8* is yet another work whose purpose is to engage us in a process that will lead us out of the darkness of our ego- and anthropocentric ignorance. To do so, *The Making of the Representative for Planet 8* defamiliarizes the fabric of reality itself by describing it through the double lens of particle physics and Eastern mysticism. Although Lessing is not the first to find a correlation between physics and philosophy, it is still quite a violation of our sense of everyday reality to see it described in these alien terms.[3] If coping with these metaphors were not enough, we are also asked to accept an additional violation of common sense, as Planet 8, in all its alienness, is still recognizable as the planet earth—thus giving us yet another world that is apparently co-existent with our own.[4]

These two problems—having to cope with concepts that violate our view of reality and having to cope with the fact that earth has been transformed into several other worlds all at the same time—are not unrelated. If we look briefly at the series so far, we can begin to see the relationship. Each novel, as we have seen, defamiliarizes things from a slightly different angle, while always referring quite clearly to earth. The problem comes when we try to hold all these defamiliarizations in our mind at once. For example, having understood in the first novel that Shikasta *is* earth, we are stumped by where to place the events of the second novel, because we *know* that the so-called zones of *Marriages* are nowhere on earth, yet the behavior and problems of these people we clearly recognize as reflecting our own. Because *Shikasta* defamiliarizes history writ large and *Marriages* defamiliarizes it writ small, when the two novels are read separately they do not trouble us as much as when they are read as part of an ongoing series—a problem that is compounded as the series progresses. For when we pick up *The Sirian Experiments* we see earth again defamiliarized as Shikasta and no mention of the six zones.

When we get to the fourth novel, if we have been at all successful in balancing the earlier contradictions, we have to start all over again in order to accommodate yet another facet into our kaleidoscopic view of reality. For these worlds—Shikasta, the contiguous zones, and Planet 8—as different as they might be, all do point back to earth. Thus what we know as one world has burgeoned by the fourth novel of the series into three separate but co-existing worlds. In other words, just as each novel troubles our view of reality on its own, the series as a whole troubles it too—by a process of accretion and one of opposition. The accretion takes place as we continue to add various versions of reality to a list that is already too long by the end of the first novel. The opposition takes place as we try to balance those alternate versions of reality that are self-contradictory. The problem of conflicting realities would soon disappear if Lessing were not continually defamiliarizing this world, if she were not continually pointing back to what we know of life on earth. But because she is, the problem does not go away. Nor should it, as it is simply another level of paradox with which Lessing wants to trouble us.

And given the relationship of Lessing's ideas to modern physics, it is only appropriate that this is the same kind of situation found in quantum mechanics, where contradictions and uncertainties are a fact of life. The best known of these paradoxes is the fact that under certain experimental conditions electrons behave as particles and under others they behave as waves. In describing what takes place in these experiments, Werner Heisenberg identified what he called the "principle of indeterminancy" or "uncertainty," by which he meant to suggest the unpredictability of subnuclear particles and the role of the observing apparatus in determining the outcome of the experiment.[5] That is, a subatomic particle's position and its momentum cannot be measured simultaneously with any degree of precision. As Heisenberg himself puts it, "One could speak of the position and of the velocity of an electron as in Newtonian mechanics and one could observe and measure these quantities. But one could not fix both quantities simultaneously with an arbitrarily high accuracy" (Heisenberg, 42). Subjectivity enters the picture as an issue because in subatomic experiments there is necessarily an interaction between the observer and the observed, an interaction that disturbs that which is being observed. Furthermore, there is "a subjective element in the description of atomic events, since the measuring device has been constructed by the observer, and we have to remember that what we observe is not nature in itself but nature exposed to our method of questioning" (Heisenberg, 58).

Another way of describing the particle-wave paradox is Neils Bohr's concept of "complementarity," in which "the two pictures—particle picture and wave picture" can be regarded "as two complementary descriptions of the same reality."[6] Because something cannot be at the same time both a particle and a wave, the two pictures contradict one another, yet in the information they provide they also complement one another. Bohr also used his term to describe the fact that the knowledge "of the position of a particle is complementary to the knowledge of its velocity or momentum. If we know the one with high accuracy we cannot know the other with high accuracy" (Heisenberg, 50). Much like Lessing herself, Heisenberg takes these ideas and uses them to raise the hope of a "world of potentialities or possibilities" (Heisenberg, 186), wherein we can move toward political unification without the loss of "different cultural traditions" (Heisenberg, 206). In *Wholeness and the Implicate Order*, David Bohm goes even farther in his application of physics to philosophy, taking as his theme "the unbroken wholeness of the totality of existence as an undivided flowing movement without borders"—this in spite of (or perhaps because of) the inherent paradoxes in the system.[7] It is Bohm's thesis that what we see as manifestations of the cosmos are simply fragmentary aspects of an unanalyzable (implicit) whole lying behind and beyond our imperfect knowledge and incomplete theories. This is a whole "in which analysis into separate but interacting parts is not relevant" (Bohm, 143).

Given that this is an exceedingly brief and simplified account of modern physics, it is still easy to see how its concepts apply to *The Making of the Representative for Planet 8*. One immediate application (and others will follow) is the fact that this novel asks us to see both this planet and Shikasta as two legitimate, co-existing defamiliarized versions of life on earth. Both versions contradict each other yet both complement each other also—a situation that suggests that these two worlds are, like the facts and theories mentioned by Bohm, fragmentary manifestations of a hidden indivisible world. It also implies the possibility that the universe consists of multiple dimensions beyond imagining—a possibility advocated by John Gribbin in his well-known history of quantum mechanics, *In Search of Schrödinger's Cat*.[8] This is all to say that the experience of reading a text on modern physics is similar to reading Lessing's novel, as both subject us to violations of everyday reality. For in its conflict with *Shikasta* and in its own story line, *Planet 8* asks us to see the oneness of the world in all its apparent oppositions. Like many physicists, this novel also urges us to give up our obsession with individual differences and accept our mutuality and oneness. The novel makes its case for change by describing a world that is facing imminent natural disaster, a disaster that in its potential for destroying all life is clearly intended to defamiliarize our own potential for self-destruction.

As the story opens, Planet 8, once a world without winter, is about to be locked in a global ice age that will destroy all life forms. At first the people avoid thinking about the consequences of this catastrophe because Canopus has promised to save them by transporting them to Rohanda. But when Rohanda is wracked by its "dis-aster" and transformed almost overnight into Shikasta, Canopus is forced to change its plans for evacuating Planet 8. In the meantime, to keep the ice under control, Canopus instructs the people to build a great wall around their planet. But this strategy turns out to be a kind of Maginot Line, incapable of stopping the encroachment of the ice. Symbolically, this wall suggests the vice that grips the minds of these people who place all their hope and trust in the Canopeans, who themselves, as it turns out, are much more fallible and limited in their knowledge than we had been led to believe from previous novels. At the same time this ill-fated solution suggests the futility—and possible danger—of placing absolute faith in technocratic solutions. As we are accustomed to thinking of the term, a wall is certainly one of the earliest and most effective forms of technology. But, as the novel demonstrates, it is no longer an appropriate response to solving the kinds of problems facing the inhabitants of Planet 8 or, by extension, those facing us. It is but a small step in logic to see that what is needed in both cases is the "subtle, infinitely varied, and hard-to-see technology" of the Canopeans.[9]

Once Canopus accepts the fact that it cannot transport the people to Shikasta and the wall cannot keep out the ice, it abandons these gross forms of technology for more subtle kinds. If the Canopeans cannot change the environment, they will change the people themselves. The Canopeans send the planet an emissary, therefore, who can help speed up the people's evolutionary processes enough that they will be able to survive the destruction of their world. Thanks to the teaching of Johor, the invisible technology of the Canopeans works its magic on the people, teaching them and their chosen representatives to accept the oneness of the universe—a change in perspective that also functions to transform the people's physical existence into a state of pure Being. The same technology that Canopus works on the people of Planet 8 is also at work on us, leading to the conclusion that one of the subtle forms of technology referred to in *The Sirian Experiments* is that of the text itself. Although it might be unexpected to identify a literary text as a kind of technology, there are linguistic reasons for doing so. For example, both root words of "technology"—*techno* and *logia*—are related to literature, as one derives from the Greek word for "art" and the other from that for "word" or "speech." Furthermore, the derivation of "fiction" also comes from the Latin for "a making." From these derivations we can conclude that, although it may not be customary to call a novel technology, it is demonstrably logical to do so—and to do so without violating either the spirit of the terms or their ordinary use. Just as Johor's patient instruction transforms the minds and perceptions of the people of Planet 8, Doeg's narrative account of these changes helps to transform our worldview—thus bringing new meaning to the concept of technology.

Although not everyone learns the lessons brought by Johor, by the time the planet is encased in ice the representatives at least have learned enough to shed their bodies and become part of an enormous group mind—the "Representative" of the title. The changes Doeg describes are related to but not idential with Al•Ith's and Ben Ata's changes in *Marriages* and Ambien II's in *The Sirian Experiments*. Both Al•Ith and Ben Ata figuratively and quite literally expand their horizons, until each has learned the dangers of isolationism and accepted the principle of interrelatedness. But, as much as they change and as much as they embody their respective zones, neither one becomes part of a group mind. Although it is true that Al•Ith apparently discorporates when she finally enters Zone Two, of the three examples, it is Ambien who comes the closest to Doeg's experience. As she charts her philosophical transformation, she ruefully acknowledges the influence of Canopean and Sirian thinking on her behavior, apparently but trading one group mind for another. In choosing Canopus, however, she has elected to follow the operative worldview of the series and thus does not come under attack from Lessing. Doeg is a similar case. After struggling to retain his individual identity, he finally allows himself quite literally to become part of the group mind known as the Representative, but implicit in his transformation is his absolute identification with Canopean philosophy.

It is the process leading to this metamorphosis that constitutes the main plot of the novel and provides us with the bulk of its recognition and re-cognition. Like Ambien II's conversion, Doeg's is helped along by a series of conversations with a Canopean envoy. In Doeg's case, it is Johor who tutors him. There are two basic lessons that he must learn, both having to do with the discoveries of modern physics. One, contrary to what he thinks he sees when he looks at his planet, he must learn that the world is not stable but always changing. Two, contrary to what he believes about himself, he must learn that he is not a unique and isolated individual but part and parcel of a larger entity. Neither lesson comes easily to him nor to his fellow representatives who must also learn the same things. They fight these ideas because they have had no previous experience with any of them and therefore cannot see that they may, in fact, be both necessary and true.

This is a phenomenon described by Bertrand Russell in *The ABC of Relativity*, where he attributes the intellectual problems most people have with relativity to the fact that its principles violate what they know of the world from everyday experience. This knowledge, which we regard as so absolute, he shows to be nothing more than a product of the particular size we are and the particular bulk of our planet. If we were either much smaller or much larger, our definitions of reality would be correspondingly different.[10] So it is for the inhabitants of Planet 8 and their view of the universe. Because Planet 8 consists almost entirely of land masses, with very little water, the people have come to see things in terms of "Solidity, immobility, permanence."[11] It is only through their Canopean teachers that they were able to learn that "Nowhere . . . was permanence, was immutability—not anywhere in the galaxy, or the universe. There was nothing that did not move and change" (15). Canopus teaches them, for example, that even when they look at a stone, they should see it as "a dance and a flow" (15). In its allusion to a cosmic dance, this passage suggests the influence of Eastern mysticism on Lessing's thinking. But in this novel the philosophy of mysticism is not to be distinguished from the findings of modern physics.

In another passage, for example, Doeg describes the time Canopus brought them "instruments for seeing the very small"— clearly a defamiliarized reference to microscopes (63). By using these instruments, the people were able to see that "everything is made up of smaller things" (65). In her description of what the people saw through the microscopes, Lessing interweaves ideas from particle physics and Taoism. Thus, Doeg describes a sub-molecular core that "dissolves and dissolves again. And around it some sort of dance of—pulsations? But the spaces between this—core, and the oscillations are so vast, so vast . . . that I know this solidity I feel is nothing" (66). What Doeg is describing is the discovery of modern physics that matter is largely composed of vast regions of empty space that give the illusion of solidity to our macroscopic perception. When Doeg says that he has "seen cells and molecules disappear into a kind of dance," Johor amends, "A dance that you modify by how you observe it" (66). Johor's emendation refers quite clearly to Heisenberg's uncertainty principle, which states in part that the act of observing affects that which is observed—or, to put it in John Wheeler's terms, it is no longer possible to think of the scientist as an objective observer; one must instead think of the scientist as a participant-observer.[12]

Because quantum mechanics deals with such extraordinary violations of commonsense experience, there has yet to evolve an entirely satisfactory informal language to explain its principles, a problem acknowledged by both Heisenberg and Bohm.[13] As a result, many of its discoveries are not readily accessible to the non-scientist. But even if the ordinary citizen's perceptions of reality have not been noticeably affected, both quantum mechanics and Einstein's general theory of relativity have had a radical impact on recent intellectual history. In this novel Lessing seems to be trying to translate some of these findings into a metaphor for change that everyone, not just scientists, can participate in and learn from. It is worth noting in this context that there is no science and very little technology on Planet 8. The only influence of scientific thinking on this world is imported by Canopus and used almost exclusively to transform the people's perception of reality.

When Johor asks Alsi, one of the representatives of Planet 8, to testify about what happened when Canopus introduced them to "the instrument that made small things visible," for example, she reports that "a fundamental change" in their teaching methods took place (91). With the advent of the microscope, the people became much more self-conscious about their learning and their self-image. Looking at the "substance" of their bodies, the people "found that it vanished" even as they looked at it, an event that convinced them they were "a dance and a dazzle and a continual vibrating movement, a flowing" (92). Thus Lessing incorporates her philosophy of oneness into her understanding of particle physics. If the world on a subatomic level consists of movement, mutability, and empty space, as this passage suggests, it is mistaken to insist on a macroscopic level that it consists only of stasis and materiality. Correspondingly, it is mistaken to insist on individual identities that are absolutely separable from the rest of the world.

This leap that Lessing makes from subatomic observations to macroscopic applications is not without its difficulties, even though it enjoys support from Heisenberg and Bohm. One difficulty is the previously mentioned fact that what quantum mechanics tells us about the world violates what we know from practical experience to be true. Thus it is hard for us to reconcile the two views of reality. Another has to do with the fact that our language, based as it is on a Newtonian or mechanical view of the universe, is an inappropriate and often misleading vehicle for transmitting the ideas found in quantum mechanics. Because of these difficulties, in trying to make the transition between subatomic and macroscopic levels, Lessing is forced to bridge the gap with an extended metaphor—a metaphor that also raises the question of the existence of mind or spirit in matter—a question also raised by David Bohm.[14] She embeds her metaphor in a series of exchanges between Doeg and Johor, in which Johor tries to get Doeg to see what it means to be a representative. The fact that he is a representative is itself a metaphoric expression of what Lessing wants us to see, thus giving us a metaphor within a metaphor.

Before looking at this exchange, it is worth noting that there is much about it that suggests a Sufi influence. It is a Sufi tenet, for example, that enlightenment is partially a matter of uncovering or recovering the hidden knowledge we all have—an idea Lessing herself refers to in a recent interview when she says that "we have lost a great deal of knowledge from the past."[15] During their exchange in this passage Johor continually asks Doeg to remember things that have happened to him, implying that he already knows on a tacit level everything Johor wants him to learn. Similarly, the motif of sleep permeates the passage, suggesting the Sufi conviction that most of humanity is out of touch with reality—that we are all asleep when we think we are most awake. Finally, the exchange itself, where a master is posing difficult and subtle questions to a disciple, is in the Sufi and other mystic teaching traditions. Thus, Johor opens this stage of instruction by asking Doeg if he has ever "thought what being Representative is" (53). Then he asks, "How did you become a Representative?" (53). Finally, he asks, "Representative Doeg, whom do you represent? And what are you?" (55). To these questions Doeg responds that he only really became a representative when, after doing other kinds of work, he finally became Doeg—"Memory Maker and Keeper of Records" (54, 22). Doeg, he believes, best expresses his essence, who he truly is. Because it is impossible to "hasten certain processes," Doeg finds it impossible to answer the rest of Johor's questions and must persist instead in his own "questioning . . . and pain" (55).

During the course of this instruction, Doeg feels a compelling need to fall asleep, thus symbolizing his need to touch base with hidden psychological and archetypal truths. When he wakes up, he is certain that he has been dreaming of the darkness from which we all come—a point on which Johor corrects him, telling him it is instead a "world of dazzling light," a world Doeg himself can return to when he is able to "earn it" (59). Implicit in this passage is the idea, found in *The Tibetan Book of the Dead* and described by Aldous Huxley in *The Doors of Perception*, that the darkness represents a human soul frightened of the "Pure Light of the Void."[16] As Huxley puts it, the "literature of religious experience abounds in references to the pains and terrors overwhelming those who have come, too suddenly, face to face with some manifestation of the *Mysterium tremendum*. In theological language, this fear is due to the incompatibility between man's egotism and the divine purity, between man's self-aggravated separateness and the infinity of God" (Huxley, 55). When Doeg questions Johor about how he might earn the right to return to this dazzling light, Johor answers him indirectly by challenging his notion of individuality, asking him if he really believes that "this feeling *I am here, Doeg is here*" belongs only to him (60; Lessing's emphasis).

But Doeg finds it "bitter" to contemplate letting go "that little place" he considers his own and so he resists the idea (60). At this point Johor reintroduces the lesson of the sacrificial animal, a lesson Johor had previously acted out in front of the other representatives. This lesson constitutes the metaphor within the metaphor referred to above, as it expresses the oneness of life. It is particularly significant to Doeg's instruction because Johor asks him to recall it in direct response to Doeg's own question, "What do I represent, Johor?" (61). As Doeg recounts, Johor had gathered the representatives together to witness the sacrifice of an animal. To the question of where its spirit goes once it is killed, Johor had responded that it is in the hillsides, "where the wind is rippling the grasses and whitening the bushes" and in "the play of the clouds"—and in ourselves (62). Then Johor had spoken of wholeness. Picking up various organs of the dead animal, he had used them to demonstrate that everyone is a "parcel, a package of smaller items, wholes, entities, each one feeling its identity, saying to itself, Here I am!" (62). But this "assembly" of parts, "packaged so tight and neat inside a skin, is a whole, is a creature . . ." (62-63; Lessing's ellipsis). Doeg, having recounted this lesson, sleeps again. When he awakes this time he has learned that the " 'I' of me is not my own, cannot be, must be a general and shared consciousness" (65). This recognition on his part is followed by a specific reference to what the people had learned from the microscopes, suggesting a correlation among the three metaphors: Johor's instruction, the sacrificial animal, and the scientific instruments.

At the end of the passage, after Doeg has successfully worked through Johor's questions, he suddenly sees that everybody else on the planet is "asleep or even drugged or hypnotised," adding that this is probably the way Canopus always has seen them (78). They are described here as being asleep because, as I have suggested above, they are unable to see the reality around them. Instead of working toward enlightenment, as Doeg has been doing, most of the people of Planet 8 have literally slept the time away in the mistaken belief that Canopus would save them at the last minute. They have, in other words, put their faith in false gods and failed to take responsibility for themselves.

When the ice has totally encompassed the globe, Doeg joins the other representatives in making a final pilgrimage to the north pole where they will all die and become transmogrified into the Representative for Planet 8. The language Lessing uses to describe this final transformation, like that describing Doeg's, is a *mélange* of scientific jargon and mysticism, with the former apparently being used to validate (or at least reinforce) the latter. As they near death, for example, Doeg once more questions the existence of the human spirit or will, wondering where it could be among the "pulses that make up the atom" (116).[17] After they die, they all look back on their bodies and see them as being a "frail lattice of the atomic structure" (117). But even as they watch, "the fabric of the atomic structure" falls apart and they see "how the atoms and the molecules were losing their associations with each other, and were melding with the substance of the mountain" (118). With their corporeal bodies discarded and disintegrating, they discover that they are achieving a new kind of integration among themselves and that furthermore this new entity has a kind of material existence, one that is composed of "patterns of matter, matter of a kind, since everything is—webs of matter or substance or something tangible, though sliding and intermingling and always becoming smaller and smaller" (118). Although the text hedges a bit on the exact particulars of their discovery, it seems to indicate that their new materiality consists of "feelings, and thought, and will"—this even though they had previously believed that in their "old being there had seemed no home or place for them" (118). Accompanying their feelings and thoughts is everything they have ever done—all their "functions and the capacities of [their] work were in the substance of these new beings, this Being" (119). At this point Lessing relinquishes the language of science altogether and draws instead on the metaphors of mysticism.

Trying to convey the paradoxical situation of the co-existence of the many in the One, Lessing borrows Sufi metaphors, describing the Representative as moving upward "like a shoal of fishes or a flock of birds; one, but a conglomerate of individuals—each with its little thoughts and feelings, but these shared with the others, tides of thought, of feeling, moving in and out and around, making the several one" (119). Even the pronouns of these final passages work to convey this sense of the many in the One, as Doeg who is by this time part of the Representative is still able to refer to himself as "I." The context of this reference is one in which Doeg is describing the myriad possibilities in any given situation and the simultaneous existence of alternate worlds in a given place. Thus he recounts, "I, Doeg, had stood in front of mirrors in my old self and seen stretching out in an interminable line of possibilities, all the variations in the genetic storehouse made visible" (120). From this passage it is clear that even as part of the Representative, Doeg retains at the very least a memory of himself as an individual—albeit an individual who, with the slightest variation, could have been someone else. The entire novel also reinforces this interpretation as it consists of his retrospective account of how the Representative came into being. That the Representative itself is both singular and plural is also made clear in the phrase "We, the Representative, many and one" (121).

Enriching the paradox of the many in the One is the question of who the audience is in this text. Where the other novels in the series have two clearly defined audiences—the audience within the text and the audience outside it—this one, like *The Memoirs of a Survivor*, makes no distinction between the two. Thus it opens with the confusing assertion: "You ask how the Canopean Agents seemed to us in the times of The Ice" (3). Of course, we have not asked that question at all; we do not know enough to ask it. Nor do we know who might have asked it, thus adding to our confusion about who Doeg's textual audience might be. Besides confusing us about the origins of this question, the sentence also misleads us into thinking that the focus of the text will be on Canopean agents, when, in fact, it is really on the making of the Representative for Planet 8, as the title implies. Another problem with audience has to do with where "you" and the Representative are located. At the very end of his account, Doeg reports that they left Planet 8 "and came to where we are now. We, the Representative, many and one, came here, where Canopus tends and guards and instructs" (121). But he never specifies where "here" is. Although it might at first seem to be Canopus, this is not likely because of the phrase "you ask how the Canopean Agents . . . ." If the audience were Canopeans on Canopus, the phrase would more likely read "You ask how your agents . . . " Thus we are left with the open question of who "you" are and where the Representative has taken up residence. Ironically, given the questions that linger, the novel leaves us with the following two sentences: "You ask how the Canopean Agents seemed to us in the days of The Ice. This tale is our answer" (121). Like other Sufi teaching tales, the novel has given us an answer that is no answer. But it has raised several important questions in our minds that should teach us some things we did not necessarily expect to learn.

It is surely noteworthy, for example, that we know by the end neither the identity of Doeg's audience nor the location of the Representative. For one thing, it is possible that the "you" asking the question is in the same place as the Representative—for how else would "you" know enough to ask the question? This implies that somehow there is a relationship between us and the Representative, but whether this is a relationship based on spatial or spiritual proximity is not clear. It is also noteworthy that the home of the Representative is not specified because the novel itself has emphasized the role of place in forming people's perceptions. It will be recalled in this context that the people of Planet 8 have trouble seeing the world as an ebb and flow precisely because their own planet appears to be so solid and unchanging. As further evidence of the importance of place in the story, the changes that the people undergo as they prepare to become the Representative are both anticipated and helped along by the changes in their physical environment. Although all the people are affected by these climatic changes, not all respond in the same way. Some turn to crime, reflecting in their own hostile behavior the increasing hostility of the planet (44). Others give up responsibility for themselves and sleep their lives away. But on the positive side, still others find that the ice speeds up their evolution into the Representative, a salutary effect that suggests a correlation with the selective adaptation of species.[18]

Not only does the emergence of a group mind at the end of this novel invite us to recognize in it scientific theories and Eastern mysticism, it also raises some interesting questions about Lessing's view of human survival—a position that recently has brought her considerable criticism from the Left. In *The Minimal Self*, for example, Christopher Lasch includes Lessing in his chapter called "The Survival Mentality," where he accuses her of epitomizing the "survivalist's false maturity and pseudo-realism."[19] What he calls her "would-be realism" he attributes to her "conviction that European civilization is finished; that its passing can be regarded, on the whole, without regret; and that in any case the hope of revitalizing it through political action is a delusion" (Lasch, 82). As he describes it, it is "not the prediction of doom that characterizes the apocalyptic imagination" but "the belief that a new order will rise from the ashes of the coming conflagration, in which human beings will finally achieve a state of perfection" (Lasch, 83). This description is certainly true of what Lessing believes, as can be seen from her recent fiction and a 1982 interview, where she dismisses as ineffectual the drive toward nuclear disarmament and advocates instead the building of shelters, claiming that as a species "We are supremely equipped to survive."[20] What form this survival will take is one of the more disturbing questions raised by *The Making of the Representative for Planet 8*, as the state of other-worldly perfection Lessing imagines here is based on what is essentially a religious concept: that of submerging oneself and one's personal identity in an apparently benevolent but all-powerful group mind.

The group mind, of course, has been the subject of much speculation in science fiction—including Olaf Stapledon's *Last and First Men* (1930) and *Last Men in London* (1932), both of which have obviously influenced Lessing. Another well-known novel with many parallels to Lessing's is Arthur Clarke's *Childhood's End* (1953), in which earth is visited by beneficent agents called Overlords who have instructions to bring peace to the earth just long enough for a new generation of mutants to evolve—mutants who are like Lessing's Representative in that they do not require corporeal bodies to exist. Clarke's novel also ends like Lessing's on a bittersweet note, as the birth of his Overmind is accompanied by the death of the human race. This development leads Andrew Feenberg to the conclusion that *Childhood's End* is a "metaphor . . . for the failure of enlightenment and the hope of a radically different future."[21] Feenberg also suggests that Clarke's Overmind is an "image . . . of a total transfiguration of the species beyond the realm of history" (Feenberg, 21). Although Lessing's novel shares with Clarke's the image of transfiguration, in it she cannot be accused of abandoning the realms of history, as she is careful to include the promise of additional changes for both the Representative and its ice-locked world. By implication, however, the history she would imagine for the Representative would no doubt have little in common with what we know today. At the same time, I think it is a mistake to read this novel as "pseudo-realism," believing as I do that Lessing is not trying to create specific new realities for us but is only trying to worry our old one. If we can take some of her images as the building blocks of a more holistic society, so much the better. But in her fiction she has not drawn the blueprints for this future. She has simply sketched some possible outlines. If we are to accuse her of any specifics here, I think we best limit them to what she is saying about the role of the artist in helping to create a new society.

The title is the giveaway. *The Making of the Representative for Planet 8* is a novel about the birth of an artist, an author. Central to the meaning of the novel is the fact that the Representative speaks through Doeg, himself a storyteller—a writer. Throughout the entire series, we have seen Lessing's narrators (and sometimes other characters too) functioning as representatives of their respective worlds. With this novel she seems to have distilled her metaphor into its purest form, as the characters in this book, far more than those in previous ones, *are* what they *do*. The very names of the people suggest this correspondence, as they change their names to coincide with their work. Thus Klin is Fruit Maker, Marl is Keeper of the Herds, and Doeg, as we have seen, is Memory Maker and Keeper of Records (22). Yet when the three of them journey to Planet 10 and return with stories of their trip, "we were all Doeg, for then we travelled everywhere over our planet and told what we had seen" (54). And, again as we have noted, although Doeg has been at one time or another "Klin and Marl and Pedug and Masson," Doeg is his true "nature" (55). Doeg defines his role as "an attempt, and even a desperate and perhaps a tragic attempt, to make a faint coloured shadow, memory, stronger," an attempt to give their "memories more substance" (90). Because remembering is central to the growth process in this novel, it is significant that Doeg identifies his role as helping others to store up their memories. The image of strengthening a faint colored shadow is also one that is important to the text, primarily because there is so little color of any kind in a world covered by ice. Thus the metaphor is that of an author bringing meaning and purpose to a dying world.

It is also important to note the development of Lessing's narrators up to this point. Charles Watkins, it will be recalled, is received as a madman by his world—suggesting if nothing else the difficulties someone might have in trying to communicate ideas that are radically different from what people are accustomed to. The Survivor is not regarded as mad, but she too must seek refuge in an alternate reality if she is to survive the horrors of the twentieth century. In contrast to Lessing's first two narrators, Johor speaks and acts with absolute authority as he is a representative of the powerful Canopean Empire. Lusik writes with the authority invested in him by the people who have chosen him as their official chronicler. And Ambien II speaks with the authority of another member of a ruling class, in this case that of the Sirian Empire. Thus, by the time we get to *The Making of the Representative for Planet 8* we have seen five different manifestations of Lessing's narrative voice, each with varying degrees of authority and self-assurance. One thing they all share, however, is the responsibility of being guide-leader both to us and to their story audiences. And in Doeg we seem to have encountered the ultimate guide-leader, as he quite literally represents all of his people and the Canopean laws of necessity. He does so by becoming one with his people, that is, by becoming part of the Representative. By accepting his part in the evolution of this group mind, he acknowledges his bond with his fellow representatives and his belief in the Canopean principles of integration and cosmic oneness.

In understanding the full meaning of Doeg's transfiguration, it is crucial to remember that his task among his people has been that of Memory Maker and Keeper of Records. His task, in other words, has been that of author. The authority he enjoys among them is not one imposed from the outside but, like Lusik's, is one invested from within. Thus Doeg seems not only to represent his people and Canopean laws but also to represent Lessing herself—especially as she has described her role as an artist in "The Small Personal Voice." It is for this reason that *The Making of the Representative for Planet 8* seems to be the culmination of her *Canopus in Argos* series. Not only does it demonstrate the evolution of a perfectly integrated group mind, but it also demonstrates the central role of the artist in helping to bring this evolution about. We have seen in her previous novels that the artist can be instrumental in effecting significant social change. And in every case the narrators have represented both the groups they address and Lessing's ideals. But in this book the author is The Representative. The author furthermore is The People. After this absolute identification with her audience, after this apotheosis of both author and audience, where, it may be asked, can Lessing's series go?

NOTES

1. Betsy Draine regards the novel as the dark side of *Marriages*, saying of the two that "*The Making* gives us, with admirable honesty, a good hard look at that underside of the philosophy of Necessity which *Marriages* was at pains to hold out of the reader's sight" (*Substance Under Pressure: Artistic Coherence and Evolving Form in the Novels of Doris Lessing* [Madison: University of Wisconsin Press, 1983], 174).

2. See, for example, her "Preface" to *The Sirian Experiments* in which she says in defense of her metaphors in this series, "What *of course* I would like to be writing is the story of the Red and White Dwarves and their Remembering Mirror, their space rocket (powered by anti-gravity), their attendant entities Hadron, Gluon, Pion, Lepton, and Muon, and the Charmed Quarks and the Coloured Quarks." Adding, rather poignantly, "But we can't all be physicists" ([New York: Alfred A. Knopf, 1981], ix).

3. See, for example, Werner Heisenberg, *Physics and Philosophy: The Revolution in Modern Science* (1958; rpt. New York: Harper Torchbook,

1962); David Bohm, *Wholeness and the Implicate Order* (1980; rpt. London: Routledge & Kegan Paul, 1982); and Fritjof Capra, *The Tao of Physics: An Exploration of the Parallels Between Modern Physics and Eastern Mysticism* (1975; rpt. New York: Bantam Books, 1980).

4. This question is compounded further in the next novel, as it too specifically mentions Shikasta and yet also defamiliarizes several other planets at the same time; see chapter 7 below.

5. For a discussion of these ideas, see Werner Heisenberg, *Physics and Philosophy*, chapter 2, "The History of Quantum Theory," 30-43; and John Gribbin, *In Search of Schrödinger's Cat: Quantum Physics and Reality* (New York: Bantam Books, 1984), especially chapter 8, "Chance and Uncertainty," 155-76.

6. This quotation and the next are Heisenberg's explanations of Bohr's ideas; *Physics and Philosophy*, 43.

7. David Bohm, *Wholeness and the Implicate Order*, 172.

8. In chapter 11, "Many Worlds," Gribbin aligns himself with the "respectable minority view . . . that implies the existence of many other worlds—possibly an infinite number of them—existing in some way sideways across time from our reality, parallel to our own universe but forever cut off from it" (*In Search of Schrödinger's Cat*, 235). According to Gribbin, this interpretation of quantum mechanics is based on the work of Hugh Everett and has a fictional analogue in Jack Williamson's *The Legion of Time* (1938).

9. Doris Lessing, *The Sirian Experiments*, 62.

10. Bertrand Russell, *The ABC of Relativity*, 3d rev. ed., ed. Felix Pirani (1958; rpt. New York: A Mentor Book, 1969), chapter 1, "Touch and Sight: The Earth and the Heavens," 9-15.

11. Doris Lessing, *The Making of the Representative for Planet 8* (New York: Alfred A. Knopf, 1982), 15. Subsequent page references appear in the text.

12. For a discussion of Wheeler's ideas, see Frijof Capra, *The Tao of Physics*, 127-28; and John Gribbin, *In Search of Schrödinger's Cat*, 208-13.

13. See Werner Heisenberg, *Physics and Philosophy*, chapter 10, "Language and Reality in Modern Physics," 167-86; and David Bohm, *Wholeness and the Implicate Order*, chapter 2, "The Rheomode—An Experiment with Language and Thought" (27-47), in which he attempts to devise a new language that helps to avoid fragmentation in our thinking.

14. See David Bohm, *Wholeness and the Implicate Order*, chapter 7, "The Enfolding-Unfolding Universe and Consciousness," 172-213. Here he argues that "the explicate and manifest order of consciousness is not ultimately distinct from that of matter in general. Fundamentally these are essentially different aspects of the one overall order" (208). In essence he

claims that the "more comprehensive, deeper, and more inward actuality is neither mind nor body but rather a yet higher-dimensional actuality, which is their common ground and which is of a nature beyond both" (209). This, in turn, leads him to the position in which he argues that it is a mistake to assume that "each human being is an independent actuality who interacts with other human beings and with nature. Rather, all these are projections of a single totality" (210).

15. Quoted in Minda Bickman, "A Talk with Doris Lessing," *New York Times Book Review*, 30 March 1980, p. 26.

16. Aldous Huxley, *The Doors of Perception* (1954; rpt. New York: Perennial Library, 1970), 56. A subsequent citation appears in the text.

17. This question has been raised in several recent studies of modern physics, such as Paul Davies, *God and the New Physics* (New York: Simon & Schuster, 1984) and Fred Alan Wolf, *Star Wave: Mind, Consciousness, and Quantum Physics* (New York: Macmillan, 1984).

18. Lessing's views on evolution under stress can be found in an interview with Lesley Hazleton, "Doris Lessing on Feminism, Communism and 'Space Fiction' " (*New York Times Magazine*, 25 July 1982, pp. 20-21, 26-29). There Lessing observes, "The human community is evolving—we all are, whether we know it or not—possibly as a result of the stress that we're living through" (28).

19. Christopher Lasch, *The Minimal Self: Psychic Survival in Troubled Times* (New York and London: Norton, 1984), 86. Subsequent page references appear in the text.

20. "Doris Lessing on Feminism, Communism and 'Space Fiction' " (cited above), 28. In this passage she makes oblique reference to *Planet 8* when she says that in comparison to the threat of another ice age, "nuclear war is a puppy. We have lived through many ice ages, through war and famines. . . . We can survive anything you care to mention" (28).

21. Andrew Feenberg, "The Politics of Survival: Science Fiction in the Nuclear Age," *Alternative Futures: The Journal of Utopian Studies*, 1, no. 2 (Summer 1978), 21.

7.

The Rhetoric of Fiction:
The Sentimental Agents

Because *The Making of the Representative for Planet 8* reads like the conclusion to *Canopus in Argos*, when we pick up *The Sentimental Agents* (1983), we somehow feel cheated out of an ending. We feel, in other words, almost as though Lessing had misled us into believing her series had reached completion in *Planet 8* when instead it had only reached premature closure.[1] Whether Lessing intended us to feel misled, however, is quite another matter. It could very well be that in describing the Representative she found her ideas converging to a point where her own rhetoric would lead her series unexpectedly into a premature climax. On the other hand, it could also be that there is another narrative logic at work here, one which is not immediately apparent but which could help to explain why our sense of anticlimax is necessary—part of Lessing's overall plan. To understand this logic, we can start by searching the series for themes other than the evolution of a new form of consciousness. If there are indeed other important themes or ideas left unresolved by *Planet 8*, then the series probably does not reach premature closure as first thought. Given this possibility, we could argue that, although *Planet 8* may satisfactorily resolve one theme, it does so without prematurely closing off others—such as Lessing's thematic concerns with language and rhetoric.

It is my belief that the entire series points toward a desire on Lessing's part to remind her readers of the role of language in determining perception. In all five novels, she is at pains to demon-strate that language is both product and producer of reality. In *The Making of the Representative for Planet 8*, for example, Lessing shows how language evolves from the particular kind of environ-ment in which people live. And, in *The Marriages Between Zones Three, Four, and Five*, she shows how language helps to shape the world in which we live by formulating our shared representations.[2] Because of its transformative capacity, language also helps us to transcend the limitations of everyday life altogether. This faculty is shown in the ability of her narrators to make new worlds out of old—both for us and for their story audiences. It also underlies the narrative techniques of recognition and re-cognition, by which Les-sing uses language to defamiliarize reality and make us see it differ-ently. And, finally, it underlies the series' narrative fragmentation, by which Lessing uses language to break through our conventional forms of thinking. In short, it is the language in this fiction and the rhetoric of fiction that set up the dialectical tensions which allow us to transcend known reality for worlds beyond.

Before examining this theme in *The Sentimental Agents*, how-ever, it is helpful to my argument to identify other themes that are not prematurely resolved by *Planet 8*. There seems to be a mini-mum of three: those dealing with change, free will, and the cyclical nature of history. If the question of language is always in the back-ground in the first four novels, the question of the changing nature of the universe is always in the foreground. It is, for example, a major theme of *Shikasta* in that Johor continually marvels at how unstable and unpredictable life on earth can be. In *The Marriages Between Zones Three, Four, and Five* the need for social and bio-logical change motivates Al•Ith and Ben Ata's marriage. Similarly, the processes of change are the subject of Ambien II's report in *The Sirian Experiments*. And, finally, the inevitability of change is the subject of *Planet 8*. In this novel, as we have just seen, the pressures of a changing environment force people to evolve or die with their planet. But even as the planet dies and the new Representative is born out of its ashes, the novel leaves us with the promise that this is not the final evolutionary stage of either the world or its people. In short, the novel implies a mutability even beyond the grave. This revelation might constitute an epiphany, but in its message of unre-mitting change it cannot, by definition, constitute a resolution. It is not surprising, therefore, to see the theme of mutability picked up again in *The Sentimental Agents*, where the focus is on shifting political structures and alliances.

Paradoxically enough, Lessing's faith in the changing universe is often associated with her doubts about how free we are to make substantive changes in our lives—given the fact that we are all, simply by virtue of being part of a particular human society, under the control of a group mind. Although Lessing is continually urging us to make choices, where she stands on the issue of free will is not entirely clear. The very premise of her series raises this issue as a philosophical problem: just how free are we to decide our fate if indeed, as the presence of alien agents suggests, we are but the battleground of foreign invaders? Even if this question is only a metaphor, it still raises the possibility that we are not free agents at all but somehow subject to outside influence—of planetary or other origins.[3] When Ben Ata and Al•Ith are instructed by the Providers to marry, for example, they appear to have no choice in the matter but must do what they are told. Ambien, on the other hand, apparently changes out of choice but then reminds us that she has only replaced one group mind for another, albeit the "right" one. Similarly, the people of Planet 8 seem to face a kind of evolutionary Hobson's choice when their planet is doomed. Either they can give in to environmental pressures and invite certain death, or they can evolve under this pressure into a group mind—a legitimate choice, to be sure, but certainly a limited one. Moreover, participation in a literal if disembodied group mind does not exactly exemplify the prerogatives of free will. So the question remains, if these people were indeed free to choose their fate, have they given up their freedom in choosing as they do?

This question leads to the question of whether or not it is futile for a people to resist tyranny, which in turn is related to whether Lessing believes in a cyclical or evolutionary view of history. Because she is an apocalyptic writer, one might predict that she would adhere to an evolutionary view, but this does not always seem to be the case either with Lessing or apocalyptic literature in general.[4] In *Canopus in Argos*, she seems to vacillate between both views, a conflict that is not clarified by the conclusion to *Planet 8* for the simple reason that the novel does not end the series. If Lessing had stopped the series with the apotheosis of the representatives, she might have left us thinking she supports an evolutionary interpretation of history. But by continuing the series on a lesser plane of worldly turmoil, she implies a belief in historical cycles— an interpretation that is further affirmed in the plot of *The Sentimental Agents*, which deals in part with the rise and fall of empires.

Although it is clear from the above examples that there are indeed several themes left unresolved by *Planet 8*, I maintain that the central theme of cosmic harmony is emotionally fulfilled when we finally see the grief-stricken and weary representatives find new hope in their transfiguration. This sense of fulfillment leads us back to the question of narrative logic. What is logical, narratively or thematically, about dragging us back from Nirvana to suffer yet another account of what is wrong with life on earth? Without knowing what is to follow *The Sentimental Agents*, it is hard to say for certain what Lessing's purpose is in doing this. But I would submit that it has something to do with the fact that she is trying to teach us how to escape the traps we lay for ourselves. Having given us a taste of heaven, she must once again show us what prevents us from reaching it. One trap that waylays us is our reliance on language and logical thinking. To help us avoid this trap, she must surprise us, startle us into new directions—unexpected directions. If we were to expect them, given our rational, dualistic frames of mind, they would be rational and dualistic themselves and thus not on the path of enlightenment. So instead of fulfilling our expectations, she frustrates them. She plays games with us, games that play with our expectations and with our language. She is playing the role of Sufi master to our role of disciple. To our insistent questions based on reason and logic, she is showing us that the best answer is no answer at all or, at the very least, a paradoxical answer, which on the surface confounds logic but one in whose solving we can move beyond the world of reason to one of higher understanding. So it is with the individual novels, and so it is with the series itself. The logic, therefore, is not one of linear or steady progression but one of groping slowly toward the truth where the best direction is indirection.

Thus, as part of her arsenal of surprises, Lessing shocks us out of any intellectual certainty we might have felt at the conclusion to *Planet 8* and does so by focusing our attention once more on the worldly problems that threaten us all with extinction. There are several story lines in *The Sentimental Agents*, and all are related through the question of how language is used to define reality—especially for political gain. One of the main plots deals with the education and apprenticeship of a young Canopean agent named Incent, who is stationed at the time in the Volyen Empire—an empire consisting of Volyen, its two moons (Volyenadna and Volyendesta) and two subject planets (Maken and Slovin). Volyen is a planet "on the remotest verges of the Galaxy," too far away to have benefited from "Harmonic Cosmic Development" and thus not a part of the Canopean Empire.[5] The other main plot deals with the imminent invasion of Volyen by Sirius, whose agents have already infiltrated the empire. Complicating these two plots and tying them together is the fact that Shammat also has an agent in the Volyen Empire, a man by the name of Krolgul, who undermines the Volyen government and the training of Incent. Running interference with Shammat is Klorathy, the Canopean agent who is already familiar to us from *The Sirian Experiments*. As his role in that novel was to instruct Ambien II, his role in this one is to instruct Incent. In particular he tries to teach him how to avoid succumbing emotionally and intellectually to the lying rhetoric of Shammat. Because the Volyen Empire is particularly susceptible to Shammat's rhetoric, Klorathy also takes on the responsibility for trying to teach its people the same resistance. His various successes in these matters he transmits in the form of reports to Johor, the same agent we know from previous novels. Klorathy includes in his transmissions reports from another Canopean agent, AM_5, who is stationed on a nearby Sirian-controlled planet, from which Sirius plans to initiate its invasion of Volyen. Even though this novel is not as structurally complex as *Shikasta*, it is far from a seamless text—as it is fragmented by these various plots and subplots, by the individually labelled reports, and by the different viewpoints of Klorathy, AM_5, and others.

Leaving aside for the moment the question of language, one can see immediately that this novel utilizes the same themes and the same narrative techniques as Lessing's other science fiction. Like the other novels, *The Sentimental Agents* has a narrative guide-leader who is responsible for introducing us to the alien worlds of the text. But as the fifth narrator of Lessing's series, Klorathy has the difficult task of maintaining our interest in concepts and premises already familiar to us from other books. Lessing attempts to solve this problem, as she does in *Marriages* and *Planet 8*, by transferring the action to another location—a solution that is not without its own accompanying set of problems. She also tries to solve it by showing us yet another would-be Canopean agent in training—a solution that is quite similar to that in *The Sirian Experiments*. And as she does in earlier novels, she tries to make the repetition of details less noticeable by using the convention of formal reports, where the narrator has to provide his superior with a comprehensive account of what is happening.

Because of the presence of two characters that we already know from other novels, there is some opportunity for inter-textual recognition to take place. But Lessing has chosen not to exploit it very extensively, in part, no doubt, because her focus is not so much on individual characters as it is on historical events and political dogma. In truth, both Johor and Klorathy are never very important as characters in the series; instead they function more as spokesmen for Lessing and guide-leaders for us. Their individual foibles and interests are occasionally raised but never really examined in depth. The inter-textual recognition that does take place here, therefore, has primarily to do with what we know about Sirius and the changes brought about in its leaders by Ambien II's conversion. But even this recognition is overshadowed by that involving what we know of modern European history, as this is what Lessing has chosen to defamiliarize most.

In this respect, the novel fits more with what she does in *Shikasta* and *The Sirian Experiments* than it does with either *Marriages* or *Planet 8*. Given this correlation, we begin to see what is perhaps a pattern in the series—as Lessing has alternated the more overtly political novels with more metaphorical fabulations. Having opened the series with a revision of Western civilization in *Shikasta*, she then takes us into the ethers of Zone Two at the conclusion of *Marriages*, only to ground us again in the particulars of world politics in *The Sirian Experiments*. Then having taken us to the heights of mysticism in *The Making of the Representative for Planet 8*, she returns us again to earth with a jolt in *The Sentimental Agents*. And she does so in the fifth novel not just by defamiliarizing some of the worst periods of modern political history but by satirizing political rhetoric and propaganda. If we had felt, upon reading *Planet 8*, that the language of either Eastern mysticism or particle physics might in some practical way lead us to the path of enlightenment, we must, in reading *The Sentimental Agents*, learn to regard language with skepticism and even suspicion. For it is language that proves the undoing of Incent; it is language that Shammat employs to insinuate itself as an ally in the minds of its victims.

If Lessing is upset by the misuse of language in politics, many of her readers have been upset by her use of language in this novel. One aspect that readers find troubling is the novel's unexpectedly broad humor, as over the past thirty years there have been many ways of characterizing Doris Lessing, but calling her a humorist has certainly not been one of them. Unexpected as the humor might be, it has its source, I think, in a tradition familiar to readers of Lessing—that being the Sufi tradition, in particular the Sufi Mulla Nasrudin, who is best known for his ability to couch subtle ideas in silly stories. According to Sufi scholar Idries Shah, a typical Nasrudin tale consists of "the joke, the moral—and the little extra which brings the consciousness of the potential mystic a little further on the way to realization."[6] If we read Lessing's novel in this context, we can enjoy the silly jokes on a fairly obvious level. But at the same time, we should look for a deeper meaning put there, as Shah says of the stories of Nasrudin, to "add to the mind of the hearer something of the flavor which is needed to build up the consciousness for experiences which cannot be reached until a bridge has been created" (Shah, 72). This is the same kind of bridge identified by Kenneth Burke as the "terministic" or "symbolic function" of transcendence: "the building of a *terministic bridge* whereby one realm is *transcended* by being viewed *in terms of* a realm 'beyond' it."[7] The bridge in Lessing's novel is in part her humor and in part the recognition, as she induces us to cross over into new patterns of perception through the jokes she makes with the language and the new slant she gives us on known reality.

Before looking at some of these examples, I want to mention some other negative reactions to the novel. One involves the wide sweep of her attack, as she apparently satirizes at one time or another the rhetoric of the French Revolution, the American Revolution, Joseph Stalin, and Winston Churchill. Lessing has also been criticized for undercutting her own role as a wordsmith in this novel. Up to this point the series had implied quite strongly that well-crafted words can make a positive contribution in helping people change. It will be remembered, for example, that Johor takes pen in hand (or whatever the Canopean equivalent might be) to convince his fellow Canopeans that Shikasta is worth their time and trouble, that Lusik writes an historically accurate chronicle of Al•Ith and Ben Ata's marriage to help heal the zones and reconcile them to change, that Ambien II writes an old-fashioned account of her Canopean conversion in the hopes of converting her fellow rulers, and that Doeg epitomizes the role of artist as representative. All four of these examples reinforce the kind of relationship that Lessing identified in "The Small Personal Voice" as the ideal one for an author to have with her readers. Why, then, in *The Sentimental Agents* is there such an emphasis on the failures of language to represent the needs of the people? The answer to this, I think, will help to answer the question of why this novel appears where it does in the series.

And the answer seems to lie in the fact that Lessing is torn here—as she is apparently torn throughout all her science fiction—between wanting to liberate us from authority and needing in turn to become our authority. Thus she continually runs the risk of engaging in what Kenneth Burke calls "debunking," whereby a writer "throws something out by *one* name and brings it back by *another* name."[8] According to Burke, a "typical debunker . . . discerns an evil" and wants to "eradicate" it so completely that he "perfects a mode of argument that would, if carried out consistently, also knock the underpinnings from beneath his own argument" (Burke, 171). Rather than do so, however, the debunker "simply 'pulls his punch,' refusing to apply as a test of his own position the arguments by which he has dissolved his opponents' position" (Burke, 171). When it reaches the point where the debunker "must advocate something or other, he *covertly* restores important ingredients of thought that he has *overtly* annihilated" (171; Burke's emphases). The ongoing example of this in *Canopus in Argos* is the phrase "according to necessity," a nicely ambiguous phrase that assigns reasons and responsibility to an abstraction (see chapter 5 above). In its vagueness it sounds like a parent's weary but authoritarian answer to a child who insists on asking why something must be done: "Why? Because I said so, that's why." What makes "ac-

cording to necessity'' an example of debunking is that hidden in
the phrase is the belief in a higher authority (the authority of necessity), and throughout her series Lessing has quite explicitly attacked all
our major forms of external authority—whether they be the church,
the state, or the scientific establishment.

The problem she faces here as a prophet and polemicist is that of
having to replace the authority she would dismantle. Ideally, in her
system, the authority would reside within the individual and not
have to be imposed from without. But the danger in letting us think
entirely for ourselves, as history shows, is that there is no guarantee
we would all come to the conclusion Lessing desires. And she most
certainly does have a particular conclusion in mind, one to which
she intends to lead us—even if doing so violates another of her
beliefs. What she is after is cosmic harmony, a realization that we
are all inseparable from each other and from the world of nature.
She would like it very much if we could come to this realization on
our own, without being told or prompted into doing so. But because she doubts our willingness to move in this direction, she is not
about to forego either telling or prompting.

As necessary as she must think this telling and prompting are, I
do not think she feels entirely comfortable doing either. Thus she
tries to have it both ways. She is always omnipresent in her texts—I
doubt she could efface herself from them even if she really wanted
to. What she has to say is simply too important to her to risk being
misunderstood. She may have faith that we can change as a species
(else why all these books urging us on?) but she does not have faith
that we can do it without her—or at least others like her. Having
shown us the dangers of the authority we are accustomed to following blindly, she must, therefore, give us another authority to
believe in—the authority of her text, based on the teachings of
Eastern mysticism that say life can perfect itself, the world is inter-
woven, and change is inevitable. But at the same time, I think she
genuinely hates to have to tell us or to prompt us into doing something she is convinced is necessary. This is when she perforce
becomes a debunker. This is when she attacks all kinds of external,
institutionalized authority in one breath and replaces them with her
own authorial authority in another. In *Canopus in Argos* this
authority lurks in the phrase "according to necessity." Now, as a
writer and a thinker, Lessing is certainly no slouch. She is no doubt

perfectly aware of what she is doing by debunking. It is precisely because of her ambivalence about the need to debunk that I would suggest she undercuts the use of persuasive language in *The Sentimental Agents*. One has only to remember what she says in her preface to *The Golden Notebook* to see how she feels about taking a text as gospel. There she says, "Everywhere, if you keep your mind open, you will find the truth in words *not* written down. So never let the printed page be your master."[9]

If she undercuts her own authority in satirizing language so broadly in *The Sentimental Agents*, that is simply part of the price she has to pay as our Sufi teacher. And yet, even as she impugns language, she puts it to good use. Although her text erases itself by pointing to its own shortcomings, the erasure does not take place before the message has been delivered. At the same time, contrary to what we might expect from her satire of Winston Churchill's speech, the text does not completely ignore the distinction between good and bad intentions.[10] Although Lessing is at pains to show us just how manipulative language and rhetoric can be, she also suggests that not all manipulations are harmful. Some, in fact, would transform us into a state of greater freedom; some would liberate us from language altogether. This is, of course, the purpose of the Zen Buddhist *koan*, the paradoxical statement that forces us beyond the logic of everyday life into a higher state of knowing—and being. And it is the *koan* and its counterpart, the Sufi teaching story, that characterize what Lessing is doing in this series. She is assembling a series of passages that conflict with known reality, hoping in the process to use language to free us from the restrictions of our shared representations. On the surface, many of these passages appear to be downright obvious and are often quite silly in their satires, but cumulatively they are intended to do nothing less than subvert our view of reality. In this, as I suggested above, they are very much like one of Nasrudin's jokes.

Although Lessing is unwilling to make distinctions between the way the Eastern and Western superpowers use rhetoric to control people, she is careful to make this distinction when it comes to the two adversaries she has imagined here—Canopus and Shammat—as, for example, when Klorathy attends an examination administered by the Shammatan agent Krolgul. Krolgul has founded on Volyen a "School of Rhetoric," which is similar to one established on

Shikasta by Tafta which "had two main branches, one disguised as a theological seminary, one as a school of politics" (55). The purpose of Krolgul's school on Volyen is to teach the students how to become immune to rhetoric at the same time that they employ it to control others. To pass the examination. students must deliver a speech that is loaded with emotional words and phrases and do so without registering any emotion themselves. Although they are easily seduced by its rhetoric, the set speech they are to deliver sounds to us like a parody of Marxism, as it is chockablock full of references to "comrades," "friends," "sacrifice," "gross inequalities," "appalling injustice," and "honest work" (60). Where we laugh at this rhetoric, most of the examinees succumb to its emotional appeal and fail to complete the speech.

Because Shammat is so clever and ruthless at using words to manipulate people, it almost appears that its intentions parallel those of Canopus—as both want their agents to become immune to lying propaganda and rhetoric. Shammat is so good at mimicking Canopus, in fact, that it even fools Incent, who shows up hoping to pass the examination. Shammat has been able to attract aspiring agents because it has convinced them that it has the welfare of its citizens at heart. Drawing on the idealism of youth, Shammat teaches them "to separate in themselves their yearning for a perfect world, and their verbal expression of it, from their cool and observant minds" (66). Convincing them that they "yearn to serve," Shammat trains them to be little fascists, immune to their own lying rhetoric (65).

In contrast to Shammat, Canopus subjects its agents to therapies which are designed to cure them of rhetorical excess. The metaphor Lessing has chosen to describe Incent's infatuation with rhetoric is that of an illness. Thus in his weaker moments he suffers from "Undulant Rhetoric" (which is an obvious reference to undulant fever, an illness marked by its fluctuating nature) and is sent periodically for treatment to the "Hospital for Rhetorical Diseases" (7). Not content to mock only political rhetoric in this metaphor, Lessing expands it to include educational institutions as well. Thus the hospital, which is located on Volyendesta (Moon II of Volyen), is officially known as the "Institute for Historical Studies" (8). The institute's various divisions embellish the metaphor, as therapy is available in such "departments" as Basic

Rhetoric and Rhetorical Logic (9). The implication is that if Klorathy were to found a hospital to correct rhetorical excess, it would be shut down. But if he hides it behind the gobbledygook of a teaching institute, it will be overlooked.

Basic Rhetoric works on the principle of overloading the senses. When Incent needs to learn the dangers of excess, therefore, he is sent to a ward which has a view intended to stimulate his imagination to the limit. Here Lessing satirizes nineteenth-century Gothic novels, as Incent looks out over a "short and very high peninsula on a stormy coast, where the ocean is permanently in a tumultuous roar, and where its moon has full effect" (8). The satire is reinforced when Incent is subjected to Shikastan music written by "Nineteenth Century Emoters and Complainers," who are subsequently identified specifically as Tchaikovsky and Wagner (9-10). (It is not irrelevant to Lessing's point here that Tchaikovsky was Russian and Wagner German, as she quite brutally defamiliarizes both Soviet Russia and Nazi Germany throughout the series.) In contrast to Basic Rhetoric, the Department of Rhetorical Logic teaches by withdrawing all stimuli. In her description of this department, Lessing again satirizes Marxist dogma by alluding to George Orwell's *1984*. In a stark white room, absent of all stimuli, for example, computers are fed "historical propositions such as capitalism = injustice, communism = injustice, a free market = progress, a monarchy is the guarantee of stability, the dictatorship of the proletariat must be followed by the withering away of the state" (12). (See also the examples on pages 164-65 of the novel.) Although the divisions of Klorathy's school are analogous to Krolgul's, their purpose is not—as Krolgul's school is designed to increase political rhetoric and Klorathy's to reduce it. Because Klorathy has already noted how cleverly Shammat can imitate Canopus, the fact that both institutions *look* the same is the key here. Clearly Lessing is warning us, through this comparison, to look behind the forms of rhetoric for the true meaning.

She is so intent on satirizing our susceptibility to rhetoric that most of the recognition she subjects us to in this novel has to do with the political abuses of language. Some of the recognition takes the form of thinly disguised attacks on Marxism, as we have just seen. And some is not even disguised at all, as Krolgul taunts Incent by calling him a Revisionist, a Bourgeois, and a Fascist—all terms historically used by Marxists to impugn their enemies, especially those who defected from the Party (129). Other examples of defamiliarization simply attack the language of administrators in general, as in Krolgul's mutilation of the language: "But we concretized the agreed objectives." To this his opponent remarks, unaware of the humor, "That is for us to say, isn't it?"—as though anyone would want to say this (28). Still other examples of Lessing's defamiliarization of the language take the form of slogans that are used to forward the goals of a particular political party by disguising the truth. Volyen, for example, much like both Great Britain and the United States, steals from its colonies by hiding behind "such slogans as 'Aid to the Unfortunate' and 'Development for the Backward' " (15).[11] Lessing also defamiliarizes stock phrases by attributing them to her invented worlds—such as the purportedly Volyen epigram "There is no such thing as a free lunch" (15). Some epigrams she updates, such as when Klorathy accuses the Sirian rulers of "slamming the reactor door after the electrons have escaped" (77). Nor is Lessing above defamiliarizing her own work here, as she seems to make sly reference to *Children of Violence* in Klorathy's rueful observation that "it is quite extraordinary how these *children of Rhetoric* are comforted by the *word*" (69; the first emphasis is mine, the second is Lessing's).[12]

The seductiveness of the "word" is shown further in three key passages where Klorathy, in order to help Incent, describes three different periods in world history: World War I, the French Revolution, and the rise of Soviet Russia. What is notable about these passages is that Klorathy fails to distinguish among them, indicting the leaders of all three with the crime of tricking their followers into heinous behavior and of doing so by the artful manipulation of words. If Incent is supposed to learn more about the dangers of lying rhetoric from these examples, so are we. But we learn more than he does for the simple reason that Lessing is giving us an alien's view of world history. Describing what is clearly World War I, for example, Klorathy tells Incent that the people on Shikasta fought for four years "for aims that are to be judged as stupid, self-deluding, and greedy by their own immediate descendants a generation later, urged on by *words* used to inflame violent rival nationalism, each nation convinced, hypnotized by *words* to believe that it is in the right" (10; Lessing's emphases).

Later Lessing also condemns the mutilation of ideals that accompanied the French Revolution, using this uprising as a prime example of how language can be misused by those in power. At this point in the story, Incent is particularly smitten with rhetoric and Klorathy decides that the only way to cure him is by subjecting him to Total Immersion, during which he is forced to relive this period, playing the part of a revolutionary. That this is the French Revolution is made quite clear in the details Klorathy uses to frighten Incent, including the detail that he will play the role of a metalworker in "Paris" [*sic*] during the Reign of Terror (48). If there had been any doubts in our mind as to what time Lessing was alluding to, this single word resolves them. He concludes his summary by showing the pointlessness of the revolution, as "the country where the words Liberty or Death had seemed so noble and so fine was in the hands again of a hereditary ruling caste that controlled wealth. All that suffering, killing, heroism, all those words, words, words for nothing" (47).

In Klorathy's description of the rise of Soviet Russia, Lessing also suggests the failure of revolution to bring an end to tyranny. In this example she is more torn in her attitudes because, like so many liberals of an earlier generation, Lessing was emotionally and intellectually attracted to Marxism because of its promise of world unity. Of its promise, she has written elsewhere that "it is possible that Marxism was the first attempt, for our time, outside the formal religions, at a world-mind, a world ethic."[13] But the attempt backfired and in the process hurt its own loyalists, including many friends of Lessing herself. In a 1970 interview with Jonah Raskin, Lessing acknowledged, "Being a Red is tough. My personal experience isn't bad, but friends of mine have been destroyed. The revolutionary movements they were working in sold them down the river."[14] One way the Soviets betrayed their followers, as Lessing describes in this same interview and satirizes bitterly in *The Golden Notebook*, was by forcing writers to churn out party propaganda at the expense of art. Thus Lessing tells Raskin that she "worked in a socialist movement which was skeptical of writers. Anti-intellectualism was rife in Stalin's Russia, and Western Communists followed that example and were hostile to

intellectuals. They thought writing was inferior to political organiz-
ing, that writers should feel ashamed and apologize for writing
books" (Raskin, 174).

As a novelist, however, Lessing gets her bittersweet revenge by
satirizing Marxist rhetoric and showing the Soviet state for what it
really is—a country that stands for "organized Terror" (124). For
example, Klorathy tells Incent that Soviet leaders during their rise
to power openly acknowledged their use of terror. Even so "people
in other, more favoured, parts of the planet . . . admired the
tyranny" (125).[15] Lessing's main point, however, is that the Soviet
leaders inflicted all this suffering on their people under the rhetorical guise of improving their lives. In short, "all of these developments were *described* in words for purposes of enslavement, or
manipulation, or concealment, or arousal . . . tyrants were described as benefactors, butchers as social surgeons, sadists as
saints, campaigns to wipe out whole nations as acts beneficial to
these nations, war as peace, and a slow social degeneration, a
descent into barbarism, as progress. Words, words, words,
words . . . " (126; first ellipsis mine, second ellipsis and emphasis
are Lessing's).

All three of the examples just described clearly defamiliarize specific political developments in recent world history. All three ask us
to examine the role of language in determining the outcome of
these events. And, by being described in such similar terms, all
three invite us to see what are no doubt some unexpected resem-
blances among World War I, the French Revolution, and the rise of
Soviet Russia. Nor is Lessing content to rest there in defamiliarizing reality for us. I mentioned earlier in this chapter that one way
she has been able to maintain interest in her series, while reworking
many of the same ideas, has been to set it in different locations. I
also suggested that this solution was not without its difficulties.
The major difficulty, as we have seen in chapter 6, is that Lessing is
asking us to see ourselves not just in her description of Shikasta but
also in her description of the several additional planets that appear
in *The Sentimental Agents*. By making both general and specific
references to historical events on earth, Lessing is making it impossible for us to dissociate ourselves from the events in the Volyen
Empire. She is also making it virtually impossible for us to think in
our accustomed dualistic manner as she is simultaneously defamil-

iarizing earth as Shikasta, Volyen, Volyendesta, Volyenadna, Sirius, and so on. In short, she is asking us to juggle in our minds the co-existence of several different, yet all recognizable, "earths."

At the same time that she uses recognition to unsettle our views of reality, she satirizes the misuse of political rhetoric to remind us of our susceptibility to persuasive language. In short, she is subjecting us to virtually the same rhetorical process that she satirizes. But just like Klorathy's Institute for Historical Studies, her intention is to liberate us from rhetoric not further enslave us. It is the grand paradox of her series that she must use the rhetoric of fiction in order to do so. But throughout the entire series rhetoric has been portrayed not just as the adversary of change but also its agent. Johor records instances where governments control reality simply through the way they describe themselves—descriptions intended to keep the people afraid and the governments in power. Yet he himself uses rhetoric to try to convince his fellow Canopeans not to give up on Shikasta. Lusik gives us examples of how popular songs are used to teach youngsters to conform to particular worldviews. Yet he is able to use his own narration to change the lives of his people. Ambien shows us how her co-rulers tried to keep a false view of reality before their subjects in order to keep them content. But she too attempts to change minds by describing how she became a Canopean convert. Doeg shows us the more subtle workings of language on the imagination and reminds us of the interdependency of language and the environment. When the people on Planet 8 hear that Canopus will save them, for example, they cling passively to this hope even after it has become physically impossible. For them the idea has become more real than reality. At the same time, because their world has been heretofore so stable physically, their language and their worldview do not acknowledge the mutability of the universe. It is only with the greatest difficulty, therefore, that the Canopean agents are able to teach them about change. But eventually they do succeed, just as the text itself succeeds in transforming our view of reality. In short, these examples point to what Lessing is up against in her series and what she is trying to accomplish.

Ever cognizant of the controlling influence of language in our lives, she is trying to help us break out of some of its more restrictive conventions and representations. By rewriting our histories for us, she is trying to show them for what they are: shared representations that we confuse with reality itself, idols that we have come to worship in the mistaken notion that our sciences have once and for all revealed truth to us.[16] But, as these novels show, what Lessing has taken from modern physics are not idols at all but the liberating concepts of uncertainty and complementarity. With some of the more radical theoretical physicists she has also extrapolated from quantum mechanics the possibility of an infinite number of co-existing worlds and dimensions far exceeding the three or four we are accustomed to thinking about.[17] And, finally, she has taken the concept of the participant-observer and applied it to her own art. In the case of her fiction, her readers are the participant-observers who help to formulate a new reality even as they read her texts.[18] What form this reality will take is not certain, as each reader brings something different to the texts, and the texts themselves are designed, as I have argued above, not so much to create a specific new reality but to undermine the old one.

In all her science fiction, therefore, from *Briefing for a Descent into Hell* to *The Sentimental Agents*, Doris Lessing has employed her texts as a kind of epistemological technology intended both to challenge our complacently anthropocentric view of the universe and modify our very definition of reality itself. Clearly what Lessing is working through and with in her science fiction is related to language theory and how language determines perception—and, ultimately, reality itself. She is certainly aware of the fact that all literary forms are examples of how language determines reality, as any author quite literally re-creates—if only imperfectly—the world for her readers. As a result of reading her texts and experiencing their multiple alien realities, therefore, we learn a new way of knowing the world, a new way of interacting with it. By making us self-conscious readers, through the narrative techniques of recognition and re-cognition, Lessing opens our minds to new possibilities—an event that has the additional salutary effect of transforming our view of the world. Once we see the world differently, we can in a very real sense experience it differently, which is to say we can change the world itself. In short, Lessing uses the rhetoric of her science fiction to bridge the gap between this world and the unexpected universe of her imagination. If she is successful, the world will never look, or be, the same.

NOTES

1. For the formulation of this idea I am indebted to David H. Richter, *Fable's End: Completeness and Closure in Rhetorical Fiction* (Chicago and London: The University of Chicago Press, 1974). Of the problem, Richter writes: "Anyone who has ever written himself into a corner appreciates, at least intuitively, the distinction between completeness and closure. Typically, you find yourself in a rhetorical 'corner' when you exploit the known devices for achieving a sense of climax too early in the work, so that you have brought your piece to an end before saying everything you meant to" (169-70).

2. Of assistance in understanding the idea of shared representations is Owen Barfield, *Saving the Appearances: A Study in Idolatry* (New York: Harcourt, Brace & World, 1965). In this remarkable history of the evolution of consciousness, Barfield takes the position that "the everyday world is a system of collective representations" (19) and that "the familiar world—that is, the world which is apprehended, not through instruments and inference, but simply—is for the most part dependent upon the percipient" (21). Based on this premise, he goes on to assert that "the actual evolution of the earth we know must have been at the same time an evolution of consciousness. For consciousness is correlative to phenomenon" (65).

3. It seems to me that this is another way of stating Lessing's previously mentioned concern with the individual and the collective, for one's freedom would always be circumscribed by the particular group to which one belonged (see the introduction and chapter 1 above). What concerns me here is the question of personal responsibility. For what is the point of trying to change if we are merely subject to greater forces than ourselves?

4. On this issue Lessing also prefers to remain ambiguous. On the one hand, she asserts her belief in the evolution of our species; on the other, she continues to show governments rising and falling with no appreciative gain to their people. Perhaps one could make the distinction that philosophically she is a believer in evolutionary progress but politically she is not. Maybe what she is saying, therefore, is that spiritual evolution is possible individually but not institutionally. For a provocative look at apocalyptic literature, see Frank Kermode, *The Sense of an Ending: Studies in the Theory of Fiction* (London: Oxford University Press, 1966, 1967).

5. Doris Lessing, *Documents Relating to The Sentimental Agents in the Volyen Empire* (New York: Alfred A. Knopf, 1983), 5. Subsequent page references appear in the text.

6. Idries Shah, *The Sufis* (1964; rpt. Garden City, N.Y.: Anchor Books, 1971), 63. Subsequent page references appear in the text.

7. Kenneth Burke, "I, Eye, Ay—Concerning Emerson's Early Essay on 'Nature,' and the Machinery of Transcendence," in *Language as Symbolic*

Action: Essays on Life, Literature, and Method (1966: rpt. Berkeley: University of California Press, 1973), 187. Burke's emphases.

8. Kenneth Burke, "The Virtues and Limitations of Debunking," in *The Philosophy of Literary Form: Studies in Symbolic Action*, 3d ed. (1941, 1967; rpt. Berkeley: University of California Press, 1973), 174. Subsequent page references appear in the text. Burke's emphases.

9. Doris Lessing, "Introduction," to *The Golden Notebook* (1962; rpt. New York: Bantam Books, 1973), xix. Lessing's emphasis. Although this essay is called an introduction in the Bantam edition, it is generally referred to as the "Preface" to *The Golden Notebook*; it was written June 1971.

10. When Klorathy tries to tell Ormarin, a leader of Volyendesta, that his country is about to be overrun by Sirius, Ormarin "assumed a heroic posture . . . and declaimed, 'We shall fight them on the beaches, we shall fight them on the roads, we shall fight them in the air' " (18). This, of course, is an obvious satire on Winston Churchill's Speech on Dunkirk, delivered to the House of Commons, 4 June 1940.

11. For further discussion of how the state uses language to control its members, see Herbert Marcuse, *One-Dimensional Man: Studies in the Ideology of Advanced Industrial Society* (Boston: Beacon Press, 1964), especially his discussion on one-dimensional society in chapter 4, "The Closing of the Universe of Discourse" (84-120). Here Marcuse contends that "ritual-authoritarian language" controls people "by reducing the linguistic forms and symbols of reflection, abstraction, development, contradiction; by substituting images for concepts" (102, 103).

12. In this respect, both Incent and Martha Quest seem to represent common weaknesses among youth, as both are easily seduced by political propaganda that is directed at their own desire for world harmony.

13. Doris Lessing, "Introduction," to *The Golden Notebook*, xiv.

14. Doris Lessing quoted in Jonah Raskin, "Doris Lessing at Stony Brook: An Interview," in *New American Review*, 8 (New York and Toronto: Signet Book, New American Library, 1970), 179. A subsequent page reference appears in the text as "Raskin."

15. In her interview with Raskin (cited above), Lessing remarks on the prevalence of oppression in the twentieth century, noting that she has "seen many opposition movements smashed. . . . In the Soviet Union opposition is regularly destroyed. Also, in our time, radicals have been destroyed by their own side. Stalinism destroyed the lives of thousands of people" (177).

16. Owen Barfield tackles this problem in *Saving the Appearances* (cited above). Here he says, in contrast to previous representations, "*Our* collective representations were born when men began to take the models, whether geometrical or mechanical, literally" (51; Barfield's emphasis). As

a consequence of this they became idols, "imagined [to be] enjoying that independence of human perception which can in fact only pertain to the unrepresented" (62).

17. See the discussion in chapter 6 above.

18. Of use in understanding what I mean by applying the term participant-observer to literature are Wolfgang Iser, *The Implied Reader: Patterns of Communication in Prose Fiction from Bunyan to Beckett* (Baltimore: The Johns Hopkins University Press, 1974), especially chapter 11, "The Reading Process: A Phenomenological Approach"; and Stanley E. Fish, *Self-Consuming Artifacts: The Experience of Seventeenth-Century Literature* (1972; rpt. Berkeley: University of California Press, 1974), especially the appendix, "Literature in the Reader: Affective Stylistics." As their titles imply, both works focus on the dynamic relationship between text and reader.

Bibliographical Essay

Although Lessing has been publishing science fiction since 1971, critics have been slow to respond to this development in her writing. Many, in fact, do not even consider *Briefing for a Descent into Hell* and *The Memoirs of a Survivor* to be bona fide science fiction at all. Adding to the critical confusion is the fact that Lessing herself has been somewhat coy about the genre of these two novels, refusing to speak *ex cathedra* and resolve the issue once and for all. At the same time, she appears to be somewhat defensive about the mixed critical reaction to *Canopus in Argos*. Recent comments she made during her speaking tour of North America are indicative of the indirect but determined way she defends her series and deflects direct questions about the genre of these other two books. During one talk, for example, she went to great lengths to defend the ancient and venerable tradition of fantastic or non-realistic literature, thus implicitly defending *Canopus in Argos* which has its source in mystical tradition as well as modern science. In an interview with Susan Stamberg, Lessing also noted that, while older readers prefer her earlier work, her new books are popular with readers "under thirty or thirty-five." In response to Stamberg's questions about how she turned away from realism, Lessing acknowledged that after *The Four-Gated City* she "went on to the other two nonrealistic books"—presumably *Briefing* and *Memoirs*. And in response to a question at UCLA whether or not *Memoirs* was the "first volume of *Canopus*," Lessing replied, amidst friendy laughter, "No, *Briefing* came first." Yet she told Stamberg that *Briefing* has a "frame [that is] realistic enough" and its "story . . . came straight from experience, because it happened to somebody I knew a good deal about."

On another occasion she reiterated her assertion that *Memoirs* is an "attempt" at autobiography. By making these apparently contradictory statements about *Briefing* and *Memoirs*, Lessing reminds us of her distaste for generic taxonomies and other forms of classification—as she does in her interview with Susan Stamberg, where she openly despairs at our habit of thinking in discrete categories, saying, "I don't think reality is either/or ever. It's always a question of interaction and extremes often interact. . . . But this, "is it this or is it that,' 'do you write like this or do you . . . ,' it literally means nothing to me. It's not my experience."

All of the above information is available in the fall 1984 issue of the *Doris Lessing Newsletter*, which is published twice a year for the Doris Lessing Society by the Brooklyn College Press, edited by Claire Sprague, Department of English, Brooklyn College, Brooklyn, N.Y. 11210. This newsletter prints reviews, bibliographies, abstracts, announcements, and short essays. As my own gleanings suggest, it is an invaluable source of information for all Lessing scholars; in fact, the particular newsletter cited here features a complete list of dissertations on Lessing from 1978 to 1983. The Doris Lessing Society also sponsors two panels every year at MLA meetings, thus providing yet another vehicle for current news and an exchange of ideas on Lessing.

Perhaps the most helpful resource available to Lessing scholars is Dee Seligman's *Doris Lessing: An Annotated Bibliography of Criticism* published in 1981 by Greenwood Press (Westport, Conn.). This comprehensive and generously annotated bibliography is divided into three main sections: works by Lessing, translations of her work, and secondary sources—including citations of book reviews and MLA papers. Because of its recent publication date, it contains no material on *Canopus in Argos*, but it does include several entries for *Briefing* and *Memoirs*. Other pre-Canopean works on Lessing are the two early, ground-breaking studies, Dorothy Brewster's *Doris Lessing* (New York: Twayne Publishers, 1965) and Paul Schlueter's *The Novels of Doris Lessing* (Carbondale and Edwardsville: Southern Illinois University Press, 1973). Schlueter also edited and wrote an introduction to Doris Lessing's own critical collection, *A Small Personal Voice: Essays, Reviews, Interviews* (New York: Alfred A. Knopf, 1974).

More recent general studies of her work include Mary Ann Singleton's thematic study, *The City and the Veld: The Fiction of Doris Lessing* (Lewisburg, Pa.: Bucknell University Press, 1977), which, again because of its date, includes full discussion of only *Briefing* and only brief mention of *Memoirs*. Another is Roberta Rubenstein's highly regarded study of all Lessing's novels through *Memoirs, The Novelistic Vision of Doris Lessing: Breaking the Forms of Consciousness* (Urbana: University of Illinois Press, 1979). Rubenstein reads neither *Briefing* nor *Memoirs* technically as science fiction, seeing them in more psychological terms. Although I disagree with her on this, I find her readings of these two books quite helpful. Rubenstein also had the good fortune to correspond with Lessing and includes excerpts from letters which would be of interest to anyone studying Lessing.

Because of its insights about Lessing's fiction and because it includes discussion of six of the seven novels I cover here, I highly recommend Betsy Draine's *Substance Under Pressure: Artistic Coherence and Evolving Form in the Novels of Doris Lessing* (Madison: University of Wisconsin Press, 1983). Draine approaches Lessing's fiction through various current critical methodologies, giving her own individual stamp to them in the process. Examining Lessing at one point from the perspective of Barthes's "braid of codes," Draine seems to suggest her own critical methodology, which itself is a kind of braid of codes, as she pulls one strand from here and others from elsewhere to demonstrate the range and development of this truly amazing modern writer. Nor does Draine idolize Lessing blindly, for she quite candidly judges some novels to be less than successful.

I also found useful the essays in Jenny Taylor's recent critical anthology, *Notebooks/ Memoirs/ Archives: Reading and Rereading Doris Lessing* (Boston and London: Routledge & Kegan Paul, 1982), especially Ann Scott's "The More Recent Writings: Sufism, Mysticism and Politics," in which she argues that "Lessing's use of religious symbolism constitutes an attempt at transcending ordinary limitations in language by drawing on a variety of conceptual and written traditions and integrating facets of them in her fiction" (187).

Another helpful essay is Judith Stitzel's "Reading Doris Lessing" (*College English*, 40, no. 5 [January 1979], 498-504), in which she defends Lessing against Michael Magie's charge that she has a bad effect on her readers. To this charge, Stitzel replies with considerable persuasiveness that "the kind of reader I suggest Lessing's fiction can create (has created in me) is very different from the one Magie fears Lessing encourages. For I read Lessing not as a stimulus to *think this or that* but as a stimulus to *thinking about thinking* (502; Stitzel's emphases). Frederick Stern's "The Changing 'Voice' of Lessing's Characters: From Politics to Sci Fi" (*World Literature Written in English*, 21, no. 3 [Autumn 1982], 456-67) offers another provocative look at the role of Lessing's narrators—one that is primarily in conflict with my own. Other useful readings of Lessing's narrative technique are Guido Kums, "Structuring the Reader's Response: *Briefing for a Descent into Hell*" (*Dutch Quarterly Review of Anglo-American Letters*, 11, no. 3 [1981], 197-208); Bernard Duyfhuizen, "On the Writing of Future-History: Beginning the Ending in Doris Lessing's *The Memoirs of a Survivor*" (*Modern Fiction Studies*, 26, no. 1 [Spring 1980], 147-56); and

Ellen Cronan Rose, "The End of the Game: New Directions in Doris
Lessing's Fiction" (*Journal of Narrative Technique*, 6, no. 1 [Winter
1976], 66-75). Finally, I want to acknowledge Lee Cullen Khanna for providing me with one of those moments of sudden insight during her talk at
the 1984 meeting of the Popular Culture Association where she discussed
"Feminist Utopias and Theoretical Contexts." Her work on this subject
promises to be an important contribution to a new field of critical inquiry.

In search of understanding Lessing, I went far afield, seeking insight
from sociologists, Marxists, philosophers, and physicists— most of whom I
cite throughout the text. Of everything I read, I would particularly recom-
mend Loren Eiseley, *The Unexpected Universe* (New York: Harcourt,
Brace & World, 1969) from which I took my title and epigraphs; Herbert
Marcuse, *One-Dimensional Man: Studies in the Ideology of Advanced
Industrial Society* (1964; rpt. Boston: Beacon Press, 1966); Michael
Polanyi, *Knowing and Being* (1969; rpt. Chicago: University of Chicago
Press, 1974); Werner Heisenberg, *Physics and Philosophy: The Revolution
in Modern Science* (1958; rpt. New York: Harper & Row, 1962); and David
Bohm, *Wholeness and the Implicate Order* (1980; rpt. London: Routledge
& Kegan Paul, 1981). I would also remind readers that I make considerable
reference to other works on and by Lessing and to works on critical theory.
The footnotes on these subjects are not required reading, but they too open
doors to unexpected universes.

Index

Abbey, Lynn, 90

The ABC of Relativity (Russell), 127-28

Africa, 110

Alexander, Thea, 10, 84 n.17

alienation: artistic, 8-9; from text, 66; women's literary, 18 n.8. *See also* alienation effect; estrangement

"Alienation and the Anti-Hero in Recent American Fiction" (Barksdale), 18 n.8

alienation effect, 36 n.9. *See also* alienation; defamiliarization; estrangement; recognition

alien cosmology, 56, 80, 111. *See also* alien perspective; alien worlds

alien frame of reference, 55-57, 61, 75, 79, 102, 109. *See also* alien worlds

alien perspective, 56-57, 61, 75, 79, 102, 109. *See also* alien worlds

alien reality. *See* alien worlds

alien worlds, 56, 62, 80, 111, 145; effects of experiencing, 11, 119, 157; mediator of, 25 (*see also* guide-leader, narrative, as mediator); problem of, 4; purpose of, 15-16; questions raised by, 12; techniques for making believable, 13, 109; validity of, 28, 47-48. *See also* alien perspective; alternate worlds; multiple realities, co-existence of; reality

allusions, literary, 64, 111

alternate worlds, of *The Memoirs of a Survivor*, 43, 45-50. *See also* alien worlds

"Ambiguous Apocalypse" (Galbreath), 10-11

American Revolution, 147

anticlimax, 141. *See also* closure; *The Making of the Representative for Planet 8*, place in series; narrative logic

Anzaldúa, Gloria, 9

apocalyptic fiction, 6, 59, 143. *See also* apocalyptic imagination;

Ghenjis Khan, 111
The Golden Notebook (Lessing),
6, 9, 33-34, 150, 154; compared
to *Shikasta*, 62-63; problems of
narrator in, 40
Gothic novels, 152
The Grass Is Singing, 3
Great Britain, 153
Gribbin, John, 125, 139 n.8
group mind, 22, 127, 135, 138,
143. *See also* collective mind;
free will; identity, individual
guide-leader, narrative, 13, 16, 20,
137, 146; in *Canopus in Argos*,
109; in *The Making of the
Representative for Planet 8*,
122; in *The Marriages Between
Zones Three, Four, and Five*,
99, 102; as mediator, 13, 22-23,
25, 39; as mediator in *Briefing
for a Descent into Hell*, 24, 32;
as mediator in *The Memoirs of
a Survivor*, 38, 43, 47; as mediator in *Shikasta*, 61, 75; in *The
Memoirs of a Survivor*, 42; in
The Sentimental Agents, 145; in
The Sirian Experiments, 109,
119. *See also* narrator

Haldane, J.B.S., 15
Hardin, Nancy Shields, 46
Heisenberg, Werner, 122-24,
128-29; philosophy of, 124
Herbert, Frank, 58
Hersey, John, 86
hidden knowledge, 130. *See also*
tacit knowledge
Hiroshima (Hersey), 86
history: as cyclical, 142-44; defamiliarized, 123, 146; as evolutionary, 143-44, 158 n.4; lessons

of, 66, 149; restructuring of, 10,
56
Hitler, Adolf, 108
Hobson's Choice, evolutionary,
143
holocaust, 78, 83-84 n.17; Lessing's portrayal of, 71, 74, 84
Holocaust (WW II), 108
humor: in Lessing's fiction, 147,
150. *See also* puns; satire
Huxley, Aldous, 131
hypnotic formulas, 108

identity, individual, 15, 127, 129,
158 n.3; in group mind, 133
ideology, of science, 5, 71. *See
also* science, as political institution
idols, 157, 160 n.16
immutability, 128
impressionism, Lessing's view of, 6
indeterminacy, principle of, 123-
24, 128, 157. *See also* quantum
mechanics
indirect teaching, 99, 105 n.14. *See
also* Sufi master, Lessing as;
Sufism, influence on Lessing;
Sufi teaching story
individual action, merits of, 86, 99
individual conscience, and collective, 20-22, 158 n.3. *See also*
collective mind; free will; group
mind; identity, individual; individual action, merits of
individualism, Lessing's criticism
of, 13, 76; in *Briefing for a
Descent into Hell*, 30-32
individuality, and group mind,
133. *See also* collective mind;
free will; group mind; individual
conscience, and collective

religious myths, 67-69. *See also*
Christianity; religious symbolism; social myths
religious symbolism, 163. *See also*
religious myths
repetition, technique of endless,
108-9
"Report on the Threatened City"
(Lessing), 59, 62
representation, 100. *See also* representatives
representatives, 92, 98, 126-27;
apotheosis of, 143; artists as, 8,
148; narrators as Lessing's, 24,
102, 107, 138; narrators as our,
107, 117, 138; narrators as, of
their worlds, 136-38; transfiguration of, 144; what it
means to be, 130-31. *See also*
embodiment, images of; *The
Making of the Representative
for Planet 8*
represented actions, 4
rhetoric, 150-56; as agent of change,
156 (*see also* change, agents of;
language, as agent of change);
of fiction, 142; Lessing's, 141;
Lessing's criticism of, 16; political, 146, 151; of science fiction,
157; of Shammat, 145, 151-52;
as theme, 141. *See also* language; propaganda
rhetorical text, 61, 65, 67, 83 n.8
Rich, Adrienne, 9
Richter, David H., 158 n.1
Rose, Ellen Cronan, 36 n.11, 37
n.23, 54-55 n.17
Rubenstein, Roberta, 35 nn.5, 7,
53 nn.8, 10, 54 nn.14, 15, 103
n.3, 105 nn.13, 16, 162-63
Russell, Bertrand, 127-28
Ryf, Robert S., 35 n.7, 36 n.13,
37 n.22

Sacks, Sheldon, 4
The Sacred and the Profane
(Eliade), 36 n.12, 84 n.18
sacred literature, 70. *See also* Old
Testament
satire, 25, 146-47, 150-52, 154-56
Saving the Appearances (Barfield),
82 n.2, 158 n.2, 159-60
n.16
schizophrenia, 23, 25. *See also*
madness; mental illness science,
90, 122, 157; as agent of
change, 5, 104 n.8, 121; of
building, 84 n.18; ideology of,
5, 71; Lessing's attitude toward,
121-22; as metaphor in Lessing's
science fiction, 15, 70; modern,
161 (*see also* modern physics;
particle physics; quantum mechanics; relativity); as political
institution, 71-73, 121; relationship of, to Marxism, 5; relationship of, to utopianism, 5; as
religion, 70, 72; subjectivity in,
124 (*see also* participant-
observer). *See also* scientific language; scientific positivism; scientific revolution; technology
" 'Science' and 'Utopia' in the
Marxist Tradition" (Kitwood), 5
science fiction, 23, 50, 73; as
applicable to *Briefing for a
Descent into Hell*, 24-25; as
applicable to *Canopus in Argos*,
58; conventions of, 43, 50, 67;
definitions of, 10-11, 44; dialectics of Lessing's, 4, 12, 59, 71,
142; documentary, 85; function
of Lessing's, 3, 17, 59; Lessing's
journey to, 6-7, 10, 17 n.6;
relationship of, to Marxism, 59;
rhetoric of Lessing's, 157;
romantic, 85; scientific prin-

About the Author

KATHERINE FISHBURN is Associate Professor of English at
Michigan State University, East Lansing. She has contributed
chapters to several books in the areas of contemporary women's
literature and popular culture. She is the author of *Women in Popular Culture* (Greenwood Press, 1982) and *Richard Wright's Hero:
The Faces of a Rebel-Victim.*